CIMA®

# *How to access your online resources*

Kaplan Financial students will have a MyKaplan account and these extra resources will be available to you online. You do not need to register again, as this process was completed when you enrolled. If you are having problems accessing online materials, please ask your course administrator.

If you are not studying with Kaplan and did not purchase your book via a Kaplan website, to unlock your extra online resources please go to **www.mykaplan.co.uk/add-online-resources** (even if you have set up an account and registered books previously). You will then need to enter the ISBN number (on the title page and back cover) and the unique pass key number contained in the scratch panel below to gain access.

You will also be required to enter additional information during this process to set up or confirm your account details.

If you purchased through the Kaplan Publishing website you will automatically receive an e-mail invitation to register your details and gain access to your content. If you do not receive the e-mail or book content, please contact Kaplan Publishing.

This code can only be used once for the registration of this book online. This registration and your online content will expire when the examinations covered by this book have taken place. Please allow one hour from the time you submit your book details for us to process your request.

**Please scratch the film to access your unique code.**

Please be aware that this code is case-sensitive and you will need to include the dashes within the passcode, but not when entering the ISBN.

KAPLAN PUBLISHING

CIMA's CGMA® 2019 Professional Examinations

# CIMA's CGMA Certificate in Business Accounting

## Subject BA1

## Fundamentals of Business Economics

## EXAM PRACTICE KIT

CIMA

KAPLAN PUBLISHING

**Published by: Kaplan Publishing UK**

Unit 2 The Business Centre, Molly Millars Lane, Wokingham, Berkshire RG41 2QZ



Kaplan Publishing's learning materials are designed to help students succeed in their examinations. In certain circumstances, CIMA® can make post-exam adjustment to a student's mark or grade to reflect adverse circumstances which may have disadvantaged a student's ability to take an exam or demonstrate their normal level of attainment (see CIMA's Special Consideration policy). However, it should be noted that students will not be eligible for special consideration by CIMA if preparation for or performance in a CIMA exam is affected by any failure by their tuition provider to prepare them properly for the exam for any reason including, but not limited to, staff shortages, building work or a lack of facilities etc.

Similarly, CIMA will not accept applications for special consideration on any of the following grounds:

- failure by a tuition provider to cover the whole syllabus
- failure by the student to cover the whole syllabus, for instance as a result of joining a course part way through
- failure by the student to prepare adequately for the exam, or to use the correct pre-seen material
- errors in the Kaplan Official Study Text, including sample (practice) questions or any other Kaplan content or
- errors in any other study materials (from any other tuition provider or publisher).

**Acknowledgements**

We are grateful to the CIMA for permission to reproduce past examination questions.

**Notice**

The text in this material and any others made available by any Kaplan Group company does not amount to advice on a particular matter and should not be taken as such. No reliance should be placed on the content as the basis for any investment or other decision or in connection with any advice given to third parties. Please consult your appropriate professional adviser as necessary. Kaplan Publishing Limited and all other Kaplan group companies expressly disclaim all liability to any person in respect of any losses or other claims, whether direct, indirect, incidental, consequential or otherwise arising in relation to the use of such materials.

**British Library Cataloguing in Publication Data**

A catalogue record for this book is available from the British Library

ISBN: 978-1-83735-077-3

Printed and bound in Great Britain.

# CONTENTS



## Section



Quality and accuracy are of the utmost importance to us so if you spot an error in any of our products, please send an email to mykaplanreporting@kaplan.com with full details.

Our Quality Co-ordinator will work with our technical team to verify the error and take action to ensure it is corrected in future editions.

# INDEX TO QUESTIONS AND ANSWERS

## OBJECTIVE TEST QUESTIONS

# SYLLABUS GUIDANCE, LEARNING OBJECTIVES AND VERBS

## A CIMA's CGMA® 2019 PROFESSIONAL QUALIFICATION

Details regarding the content of CIMA's CGMA 2019 Professional Qualification can be located within the CGMA 2019 Professional Qualification syllabus document.

You can use the following diagram showing the whole structure of your qualification to help you keep track of your progress. Make sure you seek appropriate advice if you are unsure about your progression through the qualification.

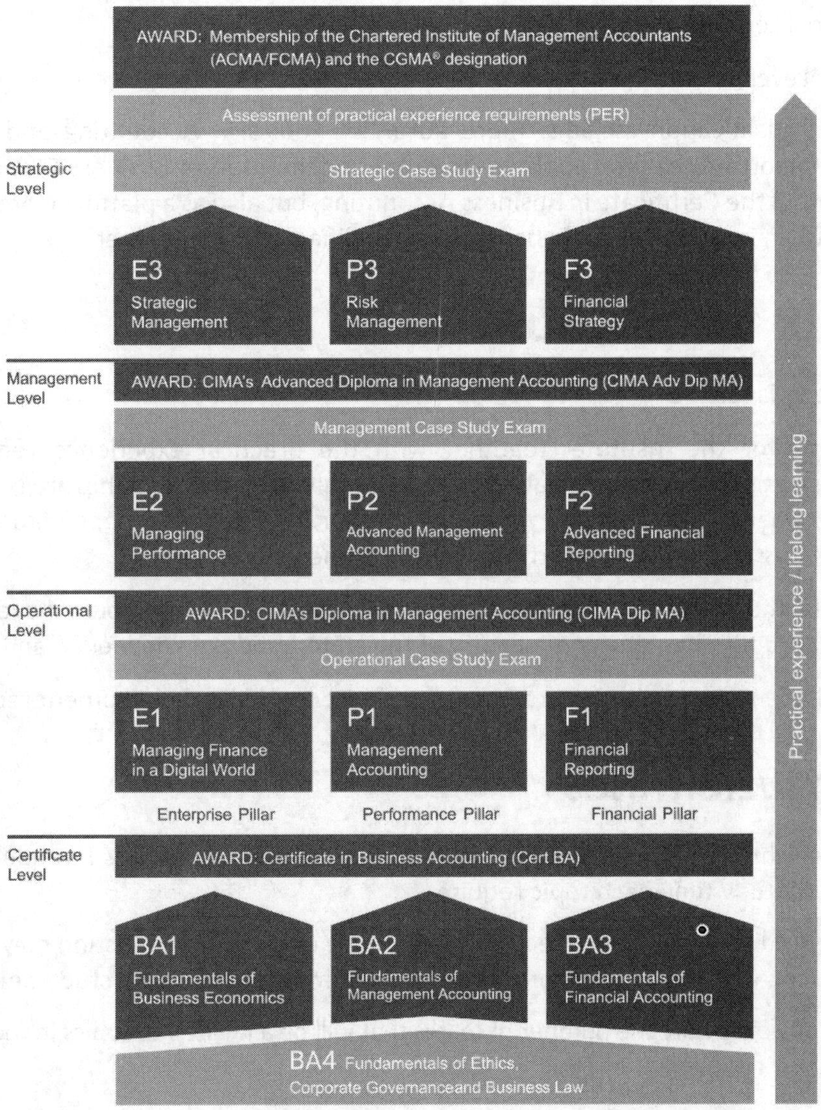


Reproduced with CIMA's permission

# B THE CERTIFICATE IN BUSINESS ACCOUNTING (CERT BA)

The Certificate in Business Accounting provides a foundation in the essential elements of accounting and business. This includes the Fundamentals of Business Economics. There are four subject areas, which are all tested by computer-based assessment (CBA). The four subjects are:

- BA1: Fundamentals of Business Economics
- BA2: Fundamentals of Management Accounting
- BA3: Fundamentals of Financial Accounting
- BA4: Fundamentals of Ethics, Corporate Governance and Business Law

The Certificate in Business Accounting is both a qualification in its own right and an entry route to the next stage in the CGMA examination structure.

The examination structure after the Certificate in Business Accounting comprises:

- Operational Level
- Managerial Level
- Strategic Level

CIMA's CGMA® qualification includes more advanced topics in Accounting and Business. It is therefore very important that you apply yourself to Fundamentals of Business Economics, not only because it is part of the Certificate in Business Accounting, but also as a platform for more advanced studies. It is thus an important step in becoming a qualified CIMA® member.

# C AIMS OF THE SYLLABUS

The aims of the syllabus are

- to provide for the Institute, together with the practical experience requirements, an adequate basis for assuring society that those admitted to membership are competent to act as management accountants for entities, whether in manufacturing, commercial or service organisations, in the public or private sectors of the economy;
- to enable the Institute to examine whether prospective members have an adequate knowledge, understanding and mastery of the stated body of knowledge and skills;
- to complement the Institute's practical experience and skills development requirements.

# D STUDY WEIGHTINGS

A percentage weighting is shown against each topic in the syllabus. This is intended as a guide to the proportion of study time each topic requires.

All topics in the syllabus must be studied, since any single examination question may examine more than one topic, or carry a higher proportion of marks than the percentage study time suggested.

The weightings do not specify the number of marks that will be allocated to topics in the examination.

# E HIERARCHY OF LEARNING OBJECTIVES

CIMA places great importance on the definition of verbs in structuring Objective Test Examinations. It is therefore crucial that you understand the verbs in order to appreciate the depth and breadth of a topic and the level of skill required. The Certificate in Business Accounting syllabus learning outcomes and Objective Test questions will focus on levels one, two and three of the CIMA's hierarchy of learning objectives (knowledge, comprehension and application). However, as you progress to the Operational, Management and Strategic levels of CIMA's CGMA® Professional Qualification, testing will include levels four and five of the hierarchy. As you complete your CGMA Professional Qualification, you can therefore expect to be tested on knowledge, comprehension, application, analysis and evaluation.

In Certificate of Business Accounting Objective Test Examinations you will meet verbs from only levels 1, 2, and 3 of the hierarchy which are as follows:

| Skill level | Verbs used | Definition |
|---|---|---|
| **Level 1**<br>**Knowledge**<br>What you are expected to know | List | Make a list of |
| | State | Express, fully or clearly, the details/facts of |
| | Define | Give the exact meaning of |
| | Outline | Give a summary of |

For example you could be asked to define economic terms such as 'inflation' (BA1), or to define the term 'management accounting' (BA2) or to state the accounting entries required to record the revaluation surplus arising on revaluation of land and buildings (BA3).

| Skill level | Verbs used | Definition |
|---|---|---|
| **Level 2**<br>**Comprehension**<br>What you are expected to understand | Describe | Communicate the key features of |
| | Distinguish | Highlight the differences between |
| | Explain | Make clear or intelligible/state the meaning or purpose of |
| | Identify | Recognise, establish or select after consideration |
| | Illustrate | Use an example to describe or explain something |

For example, you could be asked to explain the components of the circular flow of funds (BA1), or distinguish between financial accounting and management accounting (BA3) or distinguish between express terms and implied terms of a contract of employment (BA4).

| Skill level | Verbs used | Definition |
|---|---|---|
| **Level 3**<br>**Application**<br>How you are expected to apply your knowledge | Apply | Put to practical use |
| | Calculate | Ascertain or reckon mathematically |
| | Conduct | Organise and carry out |
| | Demonstrate | Prove with certainty or exhibit by practical means |
| | Determine | Ascertain or establish exactly by research or calculation |
| | Perform | Carry out, accomplish, or fulfil |
| | Prepare | Make or get ready for use |
| | Reconcile | Make or prove consistent/compatible |
| | Record | Keep a permanent account of facts, events, or transactions |
| | Use | Apply a technique or concept |

For example you could be asked to reconcile the differences between profits calculated using absorption costing and marginal costing (BA2), or to calculate the gain or loss on disposal of a non-current asset (BA3) or to apply relevant principles to determine the outcome of a law-based or ethical problem (BA4).

For reference, levels 4 and 5 of the hierarchy require demonstration of analysis and evaluation skills respectively. Further detail on levels 4 and 5 of the hierarchy which are tested in the CGMA Professional Qualification can be obtained from the AICPA® & CIMA website, www.aicpa-cima.com.

# OBJECTIVE TESTS

Objective Test questions require you to choose or provide a response to a question whose correct answer is predetermined.

The most common types of Objective Test question you will see are:

- **multiple choice**, where you have to choose the correct answer(s) from a list of possible answers – this could either be numbers or text.
- **multiple response** with more choices and answers, for example, choosing two correct answers from a list of five available answers – this could either be numbers or text.
- **number entry**, where you give your numeric answer to one or more parts of a question, for example, gross profit is $25,000 and the accrual for heat and light charges is $750.
- **drag and drop**, where you match one or more items with others from the list available, for example, matching several accounting terms with the appropriate definition
- **drop down**, where you choose the correct answer from those available in a drop down menu, for example, choosing the correct calculation of an accounting ratio, or stating whether an individual statement is true or false. This can also be included with a number entry style question.
- **hot spot**, where, for example, you use your computer cursor or mouse to identify the point of profit maximisation on a graph

CIMA has provided the following guidance relating to the format of questions and their marking:

- questions which require narrative responses to be typed will not be used
- for number entry questions, clear guidance will usually be given about the format in which the answer is required e.g. 'to the nearest $' or 'to two decimal places'.
- item set questions provide a scenario which then forms the basis of more than one question (usually 2 and 4 questions). These sets of questions would appear together in the test and are most likely to appear in BA2 and BA3
- all questions are independent so that, where questions are based on a common item set scenario, each question will be distinct and the answer to a later question will not be dependent upon answering an earlier question correctly
- all items are equally weighted and, where a question consists of more than one element, all elements must be answered correctly for the question to be marked correct.

Throughout this Exam Practice Kit we have introduced these types of questions, but obviously we have had to label answers A, B, C etc. rather than using click boxes. For convenience we have retained quite a few questions where an initial scenario leads to a number of sub-questions. There will be questions of this type in the Objective Test Examination but they will rarely have more than three sub-questions.

## Guidance re CIMA on-screen calculator

As part of the CGMA Objective Test software, candidates are now provided with a calculator. This calculator is on-screen and is available for the duration of the assessment. The calculator is available in Objective Test Examinations for BA1, BA2 and BA3 (it is not required for BA4) and is accessed by clicking the calculator button in the top left hand corner of the screen at any time during the assessment. Candidates are permitted to utilise personal calculators as long as they are an approved CIMA model. CIMA approved model list can be found on the AICPA & CIMA website.

## Certificate in Business Accounting Objective Tests

The Objective Tests are a two-hour assessment comprising compulsory questions, each with one or more parts. There will be no choice and all questions should be attempted. The number of questions in each assessment are as follows:

**BA1** Fundamentals of Business Economics – 60 questions

**BA2** Fundamentals of Management Accounting – 60 questions

**BA3** Fundamentals of Financial Accounting – 60 questions

**BA4** Fundamentals of Ethics, Corporate Governance and Business Law – 85 questions

# SYLLABUS OUTLINE

## BA1: Fundamentals of Business Economics

### Syllabus overview

This subject primarily covers the economic and operating context of business and how the factors of competition, the behaviour of financial markets and government economic policy can influence an organisation. It also deals with the information available to assist management in evaluating and forecasting the behaviour of consumers, markets and the economy in general.

The focus of this syllabus is on providing candidates with an understanding of the areas of economic activity relevant to an organisation's decisions and, within this context, the numerical techniques to support such decisions.

### Assessment strategy

There will be a two hour computer based assessment, comprising 60 compulsory Objective Test questions.

### Syllabus structure

The syllabus comprises the following topics and weightings:

| Content area | | Weighting |
|---|---|---|
| A | Macroeconomic and institutional context of business | 25% |
| B | Microeconomic and organisational context of business | 30% |
| C | Informational context of business | 20% |
| D | Financial context of business | 25% |
| | | **100%** |

# LEARNING OUTCOMES AND INDICATIVE SYLLABUS CONTENT

## BA1A: Macroeconomic and institutional context of business (25%)

**Learning outcomes**

On completion of their studies, students should be able to:

| Lead | Component | Level | Indicative syllabus content |
|---|---|---|---|
| 1. Explain the principal factors that affect the level of a country's national income and the impact of changing economic growth rates and prices on business. | a. Explain determination of macroeconomic phenomena, including equilibrium national income, growth in national income, price inflation, unemployment, and trade deficits and surpluses.<br>b. Explain the stages of the trade cycle and the consequences of each stage for the policy choices of government.<br>c. Explain the main principles of public finance (i.e. deficit financing, forms of taxation) and macroeconomic policy.<br>d. Describe the impacts on business of potential policy responses of government, to each stage of the trade cycle.<br>e. Calculate indices for price inflation and national income growth using either base or current weights and use indices to deflate a series. | 2<br>2<br>2<br>2<br>3 | • The causes of changes to the equilibrium level of national income using an aggregate demand and supply analysis and the elements in the circular flow of income.<br>• The trade cycle and the implications for unemployment, inflation and trade balance of each stage and government policy for each stage.<br>• The main principles of public finance: the central government budget and forms of direct and indirect taxation.<br>• The main principles of public finance: fiscal, monetary and supply side policies, including relative merits of each.<br>• The effects on business of changes in the economic growth rate, interest rates, government expenditure and taxation.<br>• Index numbers. |
| 2. Explain the factors affecting the trade of a country with the rest of the World and its impact on business. | a. Explain the concept of the balance of payments and its implications for government policy.<br>b. Identify the main elements of national policy with respect to trade.<br>c. Explain the impacts of exchange rate policies on business. | 2<br>2<br>2 | • The causes and effects of fundamental imbalances in the balance of payments.<br>• Policies to encourage free trade and protectionist instruments.<br>• The effect of changing exchange rates on the profits of business and international competitiveness. |

| Lead | Component | Level | Indicative syllabus content |
|---|---|---|---|
| 3. Explain the influences on economic development of countries and the effects of globalisation on business. | a. Explain the concept of globalisation and the consequences for businesses and national economies.<br>b. Explain the role of major institutions promoting global trade and development.<br>c. Identify the impacts of economic and institutional factors using the PESTEL framework. | 2<br>2<br>2 | • Nature of globalisation and factors driving it (improved communications, political realignments, growth of global industries and institutions, cost differentials).<br>• Impacts of globalisation on business including off-shoring, industrial relocation, emergence of growth markets, and enhanced competition.<br>• Main trade agreements and trading blocks.<br>• Principal institutions encouraging international trade.<br>• The PESTEL framework (Political, Economic, Social, Technological, Environmental/Ecological, Legal). |

# BA1B: Microeconomic and organisational context of business (30%)

## Learning outcomes

On completion of their studies, students should be able to:

| Lead | Component | Level | Indicative syllabus content |
|---|---|---|---|
| 1. Distinguish between the economic goals of various stakeholders and organisations. | a. Distinguish between the goals of profit seeking organisations, not-for-profit organisations and governmental organisations.<br>b. Explain shareholder wealth, the variables affecting shareholder wealth, and its application in management decision making.<br>c. Distinguish between the potential objectives of management, shareholders, and other stakeholders and the effects of these on the behaviour of the firm. | 2<br>2<br>2 | • Types of public, private and mutually owned organisations and their objectives.<br>• Types of not-for-profit organisations and their objectives.<br>• Concepts of returns to shareholder investment in the short run and long run (and the cost of capital).<br>• The principal-agent problem, its impact on the decisions of organisations. |
| 2. Demonstrate the determination of prices by market forces and the impact of price changes on revenue from sales. | a. Identify the equilibrium price in product or factor markets.<br>b. Calculate the price elasticity of demand and the price elasticity of supply.<br>c. Explain the determinants of the price elasticities of demand and supply.<br>d. Calculate the effects of price elasticity of demand on a firm's total revenue curve. | 2<br>3<br>2<br>3 | • The price mechanism: determinants of supply and demand and their interaction to form and change equilibrium price.<br>• The price elasticity of demand and supply.<br>• Influences on the price elasticities of demand and supply.<br>• Consequences of different price elasticities of demand for total revenue. |
| 3. Explain the influence of economic and social considerations on the structure of the organisation and the regulation of markets. | a. Identify the influence of costs on the size and structure of the organisation.<br>b. Explain the sources of market failures and the policies available to deal with them. | 2<br>2 | • Sources of internal and external economies of scale and their influence on market concentration.<br>• Impacts of changing transactions costs on the decision to outsource aspects of a business (including network organisations, shared service centres, and flexible staffing).<br>• Positive and negative externalities in goods markets and government responses to them including indirect taxes, subsidies, polluter pays policies, regulation and direct provision.<br>• Impact of minimum price (minimum wages) and maximum price policies in goods and factor markets. |

# BA1C: Informational context of business (20%)

**Learning outcomes**

On completion of their studies, students should be able to:

| Lead | Component | Level | Indicative syllabus content |
|---|---|---|---|
| 1. Apply techniques to communicate business data as information to business stakeholders. | a. Explain the difference between data and information and the characteristics of good information.<br>b. Identify relevant data from graphs, charts and diagrams. | 2<br>2 | • Data and information.<br>• Graphs, charts and diagrams: scatter diagrams, histograms, bar charts and ogives. |
| 2. Demonstrate the uses of big data and analytics for understanding the business context. | a. describe the principal business applications of big data and analytics.<br>b. Demonstrate the relationship between data variables.<br>c. Demonstrate trends and patterns using an appropriate technique.<br>d. Prepare a trend equation using either graphical means or regression analysis.<br>e. Identify the limitations of forecasting models. | 3<br>3<br>3<br>3<br>2 | • Use of big data and analytics to identify customer value, customer behaviour, cost behaviour and to assist with logistics decisions.<br>• Cross-sectional and time-series analysis.<br>• The correlation coefficient and the coefficient of determination between two variables.<br>• Correlation coefficient: Spearman's rank correlation coefficient and Pearson's correlation coefficient.<br>• Time series analysis – graphical analysis.<br>• Seasonal factors for both additive and multiplicative models.<br>• Predicted values given a time series model.<br>• Seasonal variations using both additive and multiplicative models.<br>• Trends in time series – graphs, moving averages and linear regressions.<br>• The regression equation to predict the dependent variable, given a value of the independent variable.<br>• Forecasting and its limitations. |

# BA1D: Financial context of business (25%)

### Learning outcomes

On completion of their studies, students should be able to:

| Lead | Component | Level | Indicative syllabus content |
|---|---|---|---|
| 1. Explain the functions of the main financial markets and institutions in facilitating commerce and development. | a. Explain the role of various financial assets, markets and institutions in assisting organisations to manage their liquidity position and to provide an economic return to providers of liquidity.<br>b. Explain the role of commercial banks in the process of credit creation and in determining the structure of interest rates and the roles of the 'central bank' in ensuring liquidity.<br>c. Explain the role of the foreign exchange market in facilitating trade and in setting exchange rates. | 2<br>2<br>2 | • Role and functions of financial intermediaries.<br>• Role of financial assets, markets and institutions in helping institutions regulate their liquidity position.<br>• Role and influence of commercial banks in credit creation.<br>• Role and common functions of central banks including their influence on yield rates and policies of quantitative easing.<br>• Role of foreign exchange markets in facilitating international trade and in determining the exchange rate.<br>• Governmental and international policies on exchange rates (exchange rate management, fixed and floating rate systems, single currency zones). |
| 2. Apply financial mathematical techniques in a business decision-making context. | a. Calculate future values of an investment using both simple and compound interest.<br>b. Calculate the present value of a future cash sum, an annuity and a perpetuity. | 3<br>3 | • Simple and compound interest.<br>• Calculate an annual percentage rate of interest given a monthly or quarterly rate.<br>• Annuities and perpetuities.<br>• Discounting to find net present value (NPV) and internal rate of return (IRR). |
| 3. Demonstrate the impact of changes in interest and exchange rates on controlling and measuring business performance. | a. Describe the impact of interest rate changes on market demand and the costs of finance.<br>b. Calculate the impact of exchange rate changes on export and import prices and the value of the assets and liabilities of the business.<br>c. Explain the role of hedging and derivative contracts in managing the impact of changes in interest and exchange rates. | 2<br>3<br>2 | • The impact of interest rates on discretionary spending, borrowing, saving, capital investment, and government borrowing and expenditure.<br>• The impact of a change in the exchange rate on assets and liabilities denominated in a foreign currency.<br>• The effect changing exchange rates has on measures of the economic performance of the business (costs, revenues, profits and asset values).<br>• Forward contracts, futures and options as ways to manage the impact of changes. |

**Information concerning formulae and tables will be provided via the AICPA & CIMA website, www.aicpa-cima.com**

# Section 1

# OBJECTIVE TEST QUESTIONS

## MICROECONOMIC AND ORGANISATIONAL CONTEXT I: THE GOALS AND DECISIONS OF ORGANISATIONS

**1 Which of the following is NOT a key feature of an organisation?**

A Controlled performance

B Collective goals

C Social arrangements

D Creation of a product or service

**2 The public sector is normally concerned with which of the following?**

A making profit from the sale of goods

B providing services to specific groups funded from charitable donations

C the provision of basic government services

D raising funds by subscriptions from members to provide common services

**3 Which of the following statements is correct?**

A Not-for-profit organisations are only found in the public sector

B Not-for-profit organisations are only found in the private sector

C Not-for-profit organisations can be found in both the public and the private sector

D Not-for-profit organisations cannot survive without profits

**4 Consider the following list of different organisations:**

(i) Government departments

(ii) Partnerships

(iii) Charities

(iv) Companies

**Which of these organisations would normally be classified as BOTH a not-for-profit organisation AND a private sector organisation?**

A (i) and (iii) only

B (iii) only

C (i) only

D (ii) and (iii) only

**5** Consider the following statements:

(i) Not-for-profit organisations (NFPs) have varied objectives, which depend on the needs of their members or the sections of society they were created to benefit.

(ii) The primary objective of government-funded organisations is to reduce costs of their operations and thus minimise the burden on taxpayers.

**Which of these statements is/are correct?**

A (i) only

B (ii) only

C Both

D Neither

**6** An example of the principal-agent problem in business is where principals, such as _________, delegate control to agents, such as _________. The problem is one of devising methods to ensure that agents act in the best interest of the principals. Managerial reward systems which link pay and bonuses to the improvement in _________ is one such method.

**Choose from the following 'drop down' options to complete the above sentence.**

| | |
|---|---|
| **management** | **stakeholders** |
| **shareholder wealth** | **shareholders** |
| **efficiency** | |

**7** Over the past year the X Co earned profits before tax and interest of $110,000. It has interest charges of $45,000 and a tax bill of $30,000. Preference share dividends of $15,000 were paid out, as were ordinary dividends of $5,000. X Co has $125,000 of share capital in issue and the shares each have a nominal value of $0.50.

**Calculate the earnings per share for the year in $ to the nearest cent.**

| |
|---|
| **$** |

**The next two questions are based on the following information.**

| | |
|---|---|
| Dividend per share | 8.6c |
| Net profit after taxation | $17,000 |
| Interest paid | $2,000 |
| Number of ordinary shares | 70,000 |
| Market price of share | 204c |

**8 The dividend yield is**

A 8.6%

B 6.4%

C 4.2%

D 2.1%

**9 The earnings per share is**

A $0.15

B $0.185

C $0.214

D $0.243

**10 In the short run, companies will attempt to improve shareholder wealth by maximising:**

A Return on Capital Employed

B Net Present Value

C Normal profits

D Average revenue

**11 Earnings Per Share (eps) is sometimes used to make decisions about shareholder investment in the short run. What is the main weakness of this measure?**

A It is difficult to calculate

B It varies depending on the profit achieved by the company

C It does not measure change in shareholder wealth

D It can only be calculated once each year

**12 The main technique used to measure increase in shareholder value in the long run is:**

A Earnings Per Share

B Return On Capital Employed

C Discounted cash flows

D Net profit

13 Employees are _______ stakeholders, while finance providers are _______ stakeholders.

**Which TWO words fill the gaps in the above sentence?**

A Internal, Connected

B External, Internal

C Connected, Outsider

D Internal, Supplier

14 **FCC is a large bank. Which TWO of the following would be classified as connected stakeholders for FCC?**

A FCC's shareholders

B FCC's employees

C Customers who borrow money from FCC

D FCC's managers and directors

E The government banking regulator

F The trade union representing FCC's employees

15 **Which of the following is unlikely to be a cause of conflict between directors and shareholders?**

A 'Fat cat' salaries

B Maximisation of short-term profitability

C Maximisation of long-term cash flows

D Mergers and acquisitions

16 **Which of the following is NOT normally seen to be an objective of corporate governance?**

A Improving employee welfare

B Increasing disclosure to stakeholders

C Ensuring that the company is run in a legal and ethical manner

D Increasing the level of confidence in the company for investors and shareholders

17 **Indicate by clicking in the appropriate box whether the following statements are true or false.**

| **Statement** | **True** | **False** |
|---|---|---|
| One of the main benefits of corporate governance is improved access to capital markets. | | |
| Under the principles of good corporate governance, the CEO and chairman of the board will normally be the same person. | | |

**18 Transaction costs are associated with which ONE of the following?**

A Materials procurement

B Flexible working arrangements

C Outsourcing

D Lobbying

# MICROECONOMIC AND ORGANISATIONAL CONTEXT II: THE MARKET SYSTEM

**19 From the demand schedule below, the price elasticity of demand using the non-average arc method, following a fall in price of Product X from 25c to 20c is**

| Price | Quantity |
|---|---|
| 30 | 15 |
| 25 | 20 |
| 20 | 25 |
| 15 | 30 |

**20 From the demand schedule below, the price elasticity of demand using the average arc method, following a fall in price of Product X from 25c to 20c is**

| Price | Quantity |
|---|---|
| 30 | 15 |
| 25 | 20 |
| 20 | 25 |
| 15 | 30 |

**21 Which of the following is NOT held constant when we draw the demand curve?**

A the price of complementary goods

B the price of substitutes

C consumers' income

D the price of the good

**22** A demand curve is drawn assuming all but one of the following remains unchanged.

**Which item can vary?**

A Consumer tastes

B The price of the product

C The price of other products

D Disposable income

**23 Movement from $P_0$ to $P_1$ shows what?**

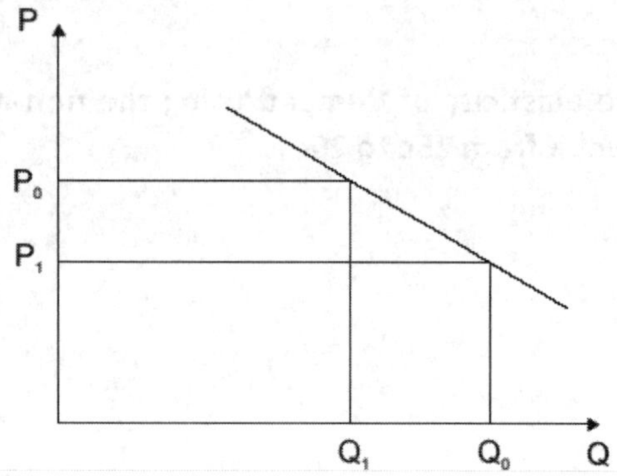


A An increase in the supply of the good

B A fall in the supply of the good

C An expansion of demand

D A fall in demand

**24 A normal demand curve is downward sloping because:**

A raising prices causes an expansion in demand

B raising prices causes a contraction in demand

C companies require a lower profit margin as more of an item is produced

D companies require a higher profit margin as more of an item is produced

**25 Complementary goods exist where:**

A the purchase of one good means that a similar good is not purchased

B a number of goods exist, any of which can be purchased to satisfy a need

C one good is free and the other has to be paid for

D the purchase of one good leads to the purchase of another good

**26 Use the terms below to complete the sentences regarding the demand curve:**

- a shift to the right of the demand curve
- a shift to the left of the demand curve
- an expansion along the demand curve
- a contraction along the demand curve

A If the price of the good rises there will be...

B If disposable income increases there will be...

C If the supply of the good increases there will be...

D If the price of a substitute falls there will be...

**27 The demand curve for the product of a business will shift to the right when there is:**

A a reduction in indirect tax on the good

B an improvement in production which lowers costs

C a fall in the price of the good

D an increase in the demand of a complementary good

**28 The shift to the right in the supply curve on the diagram below can best be explained by:**

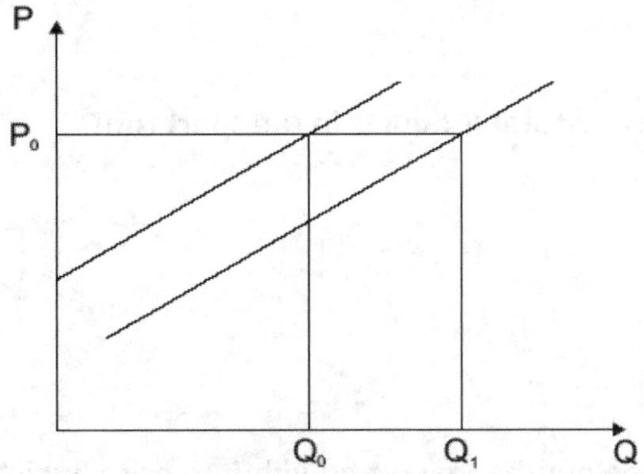


A an increase in the price of the product

B an increase in the price of raw materials

C a rise in the amount of wages paid to labour

D the result of technological progress

**29 Which TWO of the following statements are true?**

A Raising the price of an elastic product will lead to an increase in total revenue

B Raising the price of an elastic product will lead to a decrease in total revenue

C Raising the price of an inelastic product will lead to an increase in total revenue

D Raising the price of an inelastic product will lead to a decrease in total revenue

**30 Which of the following factors would NOT influence the price elasticity of supply?**

A Time

B Stock levels

C Number of firms in the industry

D Habit

**31 Which of the following would NOT shift the supply curve to the right?**

A a government subsidy

B a government expenditure tax

C an increase in technology

D lower input price

**32 A farmer produces 1,000 tonnes of wheat with the government guaranteeing $50 per tonne produced. If the subsidy is increased by $5 per tonne and production rises to 1,200 tonnes, the elasticity of supply of wheat, using the non-average arc method, is equal to**

A −1

B +1

C −2

D +2

**33 How would you describe the supply of agricultural products in the short run?**

A completely elastic

B elastic

C inelastic

D impossible to determine

**34 If the government set a maximum price below the market equilibrium price, which of the following will this lead to?**

A excess demand

B excess supply

C market equilibrium

D none of the above

**35 Which TWO of the following statements do NOT explain why the quantity of a product supplied may only increase in the long term?**

A the product may have a very long lead time

B spare production capacity is high

C the products are necessities

D import tariffs are very high

**36 In the diagram below, what action will suppliers take at the price of $P_{high}$?**

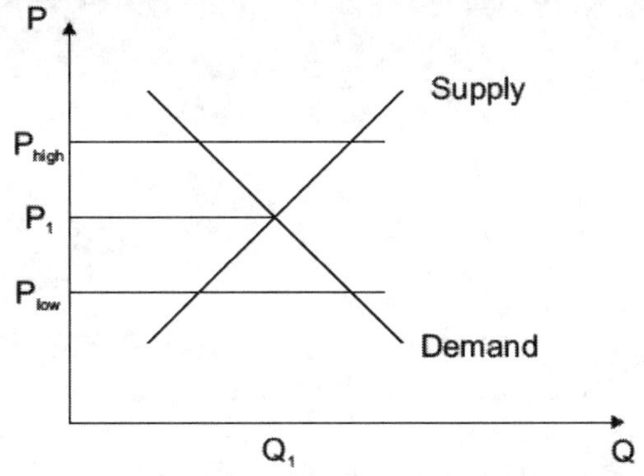


A Increase supply to take advantage of the high price

B Supply the same quantity of goods but at a reduced price

C Supply a reduced quantity of goods but at the same price

D Decrease price to attract more demand

**37 In the diagram below the equilibrium price for chocolate is $P_0$ and $Q_0$. What will the new equilibrium price be if people's incomes increase and chocolate is a normal good?**

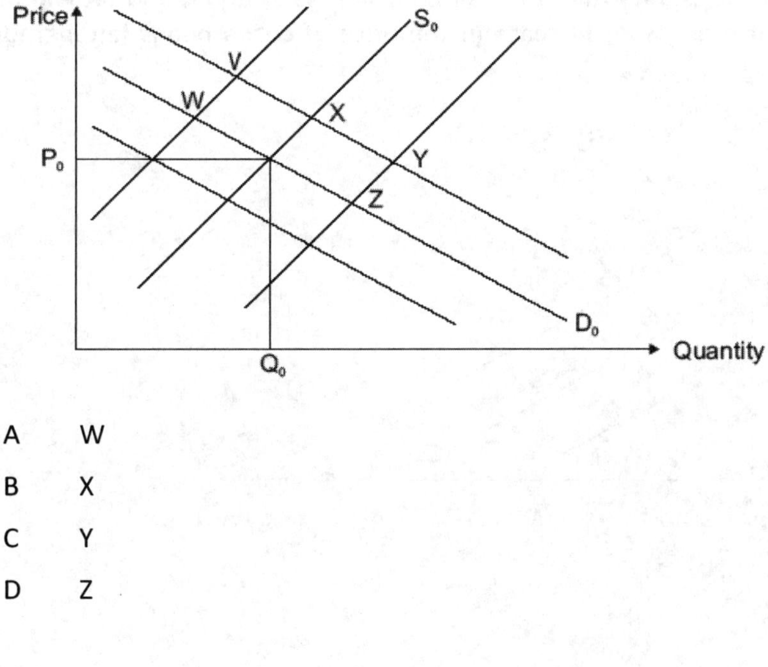


A W

B X

C Y

D Z

**38 In the diagram below the equilibrium price for chocolate is $P_0$ and $Q_0$. What will the new equilibrium price be if there is technological progress in the chocolate-making industry?**

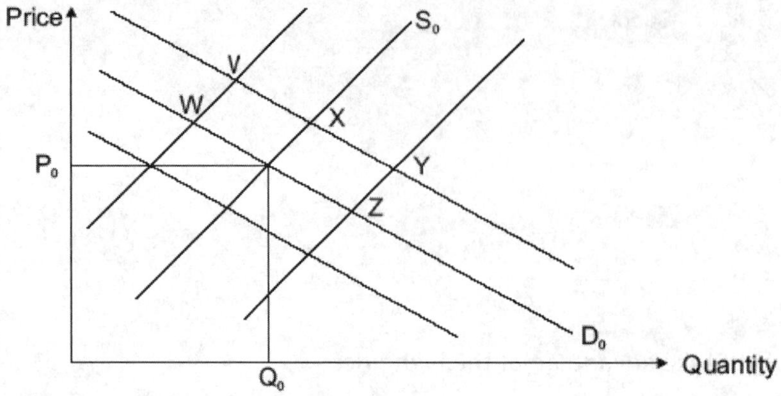


A W

B X

C Y

D Z

**39 In the diagram below the equilibrium price for chocolate is $P_0$ and $Q_0$. What will the new equilibrium price be if there is an increase in the price of cocoa beans (an ingredient in chocolate)?**

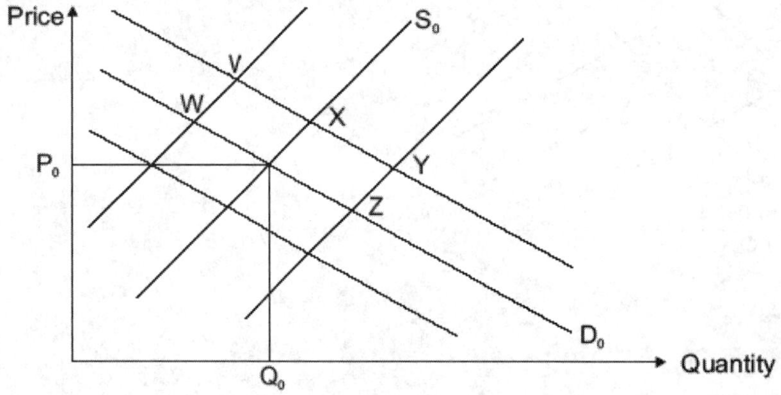


A V

B W

C X

D Z

**40 E-commerce generally increases the price elasticity of demand for the products of a particular supplier. Which one of the following statements does NOT describe a cause of this?**

A greater availability of substitutes from a market with more participants

B generally lower prices due to search engines

C lower cost of search for alternatives

D greater focus on price due to e-commerce reducing opportunities for differentiation of service

**41 Which of the following goods is most likely to experience large fluctuations in supply due to the lag between change in prices and producers responding to that change?**

A Motor vehicles

B Air travel

C Mobile telephones

D Wheat

**42 A rise in the price of a good accompanied by a fall in the quantity sold would result from:**

A decrease in supply

B increase in demand

C decrease in demand

D increase in supply

**43 If a firm is enjoying economies of scale, then**

A it is suffering from excess capacity

B it must be a monopoly

C it is maximising profits

D unit cost is falling as output rises

**44 The main benefit of specialisation of labour to a company is that it:**

A creates economies of scale

B raises the productivity of labour

C reduces the boredom involved in manual work

D generates product differentiation

**45 Which of the following is an example of an external economy of scale for a business enterprise?**

A A locally available trained labour force

B Technical economies of scale

C Bulk buying

D Financial economies of scale

**46 Which of the following are external economies of scale for a business enterprise?**

(i) A locally available trained labour force.

(ii) The presence of specialist firms providing components.

(iii) The ability of larger firms to secure cheaper bank loans.

(iv) The development of specialised transport and communications facilities.

A (i), (ii) and (iii) only

B (ii), (iii) and (iv) only

C (i), (ii) and (iv) only

D (i), (iii) and (iv) only

**47 Economies of scale:**

A can be gained only by monopoly firms

B are possible only if there is a sufficient demand for the product

C do not necessarily reduce unit costs of production

D depend on the efficiency of management

**48 Which of the following would be an example of a merit good?**

(i) Healthcare

(ii) Education

(iii) Road Congestion

A (i)

B (ii)

C (iii)

D (i) and (ii)

**49 Why are public goods produced in the public sector?**

A They are characterised by non-excludability and non-exclusivity

B They have high initial capital costs for production

C They are examples of natural monopolies

D Their production and consumption involves significant external benefits

**50 Which of the following is a description of a pure public good?**

A no individual can be excluded from consuming it

B when consumed by one person implies less consumption by others

C involves no social costs in production

D is produced by the state

**51 Which is the following will result from a chemical company reducing the level of pollution from its factory.**

A a fall in social costs

B a fall in social benefits

C a fall in average costs

D a fall in marginal costs

**52 Which TWO of the following are examples of merit goods?**

A defence

B health

C education

D water

**53 Which of the following is NOT an argument in favour of privatisation?**

A a reduction in bureaucracy

B a more even distribution of income and wealth

C increased competition between firms in the same industry

D greater consumer choice

**54 Which one of the following is NOT a valid economic reason for producing goods and services by the state?**

A it is a merit good

B it is a public good

C it is a natural monopoly

D it is a necessity which is consumed by everyone

**55 When privatisation takes place**

A assets are transferred from the public sector and money goes to the government

B assets are transferred from the private sector and money goes to the government

C assets are transferred from the private sector and money goes to the private sector

D assets are transferred from the public sector and money goes to the private sector

**56 The production of a good results in a positive externality. Which of the following actions would you recommend the government should take?**

A give the producer a subsidy which reflects the marginal benefit from the consumption of the good

B give the producer a subsidy which reflects the marginal cost of the externality

C impose a tax on the producer which reflects the marginal benefit derived from consumption

D impose a tax on the producer which reflects the marginal cost of the externality

**57 The government may discourage horizontal mergers in manufacturing industry because**

A by controlling the sources of supply, the merged firms will have unfair advantages over its rivals

B the merged firms will be unable to secure economies of scale

C consumers may lose out if the merged firm acquires market dominance

D there is a lack of synergy between the two companies

**58 Which of the following is NOT a tool that the government can use to attempt to stabilise markets?**

A Setting minimum prices

B Providing guaranteed minimum income for producers in the market

C Preventing over-production through set-aside payments

D Setting a minimum wage

**59 Which ONE of the following best describes the main purposes of organisation such as the Competition Commission in the UK?**

A To prevent the growth of large firms

B To investigate anti-competitive behaviour by firms

C To encourage mergers to enable firms to secure economies of scale

D To regulate the prices charged by privatised utilities

**60 Which ONE of the following would be a sound economic reason for a government to prevent a merger between two companies?**

A Combined profits would increase

B Competition would decrease and prices would rise

C The industry would become more concentrated

D The companies are operating in the same industry

**61 Demand for a product is 1,000 units when the price is set at $100. The product has a price elasticity of demand (PED) of -1.5 when calculated using the non-average arc method. What will demand for the product become if the price is increased by 10%?**

A 850 units

B 900 units

C 1,100 units

D 1,500 units

**62 Demand for a product is 22,300 units when the price is set at $3.50. The product has a price elasticity of demand (PED) of -0.8 when calculated using the non-average arc method. What will demand for the product become (in units to the nearest whole unit) if the price is decreased by 8%?**

| | |
|---|---|
| | **units** |

**63 Demand for a product is 40,000 units when the price is set at $60. The product has a price elasticity of demand (PED) of -1.2 when calculated using the non-average arc method. The sales manager has suggested lowering the price to stimulate demand to 50,000 units to make use of production capacity and economies of scale. What price should be charged, in $ to the nearest whole $, to achieve demand of 50,000 units?**

| | |
|---|---|
| **$** | |

**64 A company supplies 12,000 units of a product when its sales price is set at $50. The product has a price elasticity of supply (PES) of +1.4 when calculated using the non-average arc method. How many units of the product will the company aim to supply if the sales price grows by 5%?**

A 12,480 units

B 12,600 units

C 12,840 units

D 16,800 units

# FINANCIAL CONTEXT OF BUSINESS I

**65 Indicate by clicking in the appropriate box whether the following statements are true or false.**

| **Statement** | **True** | **False** |
|---|---|---|
| Coupon bearing securities have a fixed maturity and a specified rate of interest | | |
| In the discount market, funds are raised by issuing bills at a discount to their eventual redemption or maturity value | | |

**66 Which THREE of the following are key roles played by money markets?**

A Providing short-term liquidity to companies, banks and the public sector

B Providing short term trade finance

C Allowing an organisation to manage its exposure to foreign currency risk and interest rate risk

D Dealing in long-term funds and transactions

**67 Which of the following are money market instruments?**

1 Certificates of deposit

2 Corporate bond

3 Commercial paper

4 Treasury bill

A 1, 2 and 4 only

B 1 and 3 only

C 1, 3 and 4 only

D 1, 2 and 3 and 4

**68 Which of the following is a difference between primary and secondary capital markets?**

A Primary capital markets relate to the sale of new securities, while secondary capital markets are where securities trade after their initial offering.

B Both primary and secondary capital markets relate to where securities are traded after their initial offering.

C Both primary and secondary capital markets relate to the sale of new securities.

D Primary markets are where stocks trade and secondary markets are where loan notes trade.

**69 Which THREE of the following are true, in relation to certificates of deposit?**

A They are evidence of a deposit with an issuing bank

B They are not negotiable and therefore unattractive to the depositor as they do not ensure instant liquidity

C They provide the bank with a deposit for a fixed period at a fixed rate of interest

D They are coupon-bearing securities

**70 If the central bank raised interest rates, the most likely outcome on the stock market would be?**

A A rise in share prices

B A fall in share prices

C No change in share prices

D Impossible to tell

**71** **If a central bank pursues an expansionary open market operations policy, it will carry out which of the following?**

A sell securities on the open market

B buy securities from non-government holders

C increase the reverse asset ratio

D decrease the reserve asset ratio

**72** **Which of the following is never an asset of a clearing bank?**

A cash

B loans made to a company

C a customer's deposit account

D balances held with the Bank of England

**73** **If the reserve asset ratio was 25%, how much money could a bank create from an initial deposit of $100?**

A $100

B $200

C $300

D $400

**74** **ABC Co has made a new issue of redeemable bonds. If the market rate of interest falls, how will the price of the bonds react?**

A rise

B fall

C stay the same

D could go up or down

**75** **Lenders normally want to lend funds for a short period of time, but most borrowers want to borrow funds for a long period of time. How would you describe the solving of this mismatch?**

A pooling

B aggregation

C risk reduction

D maturity transformation

**76** **What is the main reason that borrowers and lenders are unlikely to contact each other directly?**

A Lack of communication systems

B High costs

C Financial intermediaries are only open for a limited amount of time each day

D They are unlikely to have assets that can be traded

**77** **What is the main way of distinguishing between capital and money markets?**

A transaction costs

B the amounts involved

C the time to maturity

D the amount of risk

**78** **Which of the following does NOT engage in the buying and selling of shares in other companies?**

A Unit trusts

B Investment trusts

C Pension funds

D The Stock Exchange

**79** **Which of the following statements is FALSE regarding ordinary shares?**

A They carry higher risk for the investor relative to bonds issued by the same company

B Dividends are paid at the discretion of the company

C Unquoted company shares are less liquid than those of quoted companies

D Ordinary shares are redeemable by the company at the discretion of the investor

**80** **Which of the following is NOT a function of the World Trade Organisation (WTO)?**

A providing finance for countries with a balance of payments deficit

B encouraging countries to reduce tariffs

C encouraging free trade areas

D discouraging non-tariff barriers

**81** Assume that the current market rate of interest is 5%. The government is issuing new bonds at $100 each offering a yield at 5%.

**If the market interest rate fell to 2%, what would be the maximum price a rational investor would pay for the bond?**

A $40

B $100

C $200

D $250

# MACROECONOMIC AND INSTITUTIONAL CONTEXT I: THE DOMESTIC ECONOMY

**82 Which of the following are included in aggregate demand? Indicate your answer by ticking in the appropriate box.**

| | **Included** | **Not included** |
|---|---|---|
| Consumption | | |
| Income | | |
| Savings | | |
| Investment | | |

**83 A leftward shift in the supply curve while demand is unchanged would lead to which of the following?**

A rising prices and lower output

B rising prices higher output

C falling prices and lower output

D falling prices and higher output

**84** Consider the following information.

| | | $m |
|---|---|---|
| Exports | (X) | 432 |
| Investment | (I) | 249 |
| Savings | (S) | 176 |
| Government expenditure | (G) | 329 |
| Imports | (M) | 503 |
| Taxes | (T) | 298 |

**The national income of this economy will**

A start to fall

B start to rise

C remain static

D be in equilibrium

**85 The figures below show the consumption function for a given economy.**

| Income | Consumption |
|---|---|
| $m | $m |
| 100 | 95 |
| 120 | 110 |
| 140 | 125 |
| 160 | 140 |
| 180 | 155 |

The value of the MPC in this economy is

[ ]

**86 A closed economy with no government sector has a marginal propensity to consume of 0.8 and a full employment level of $100 million. The current level of national income is $80 million. To achieve full employment, investment must rise by**

A $4 million

B $8 million

C $16 million

D $20 million

**87 Which of the following situations would lead to the existence of a deflationary gap?**

A there has been a general fall in prices

B planned expenditure exceeds the full employment level of output

C planned expenditure is below the full employment level of output

D the time it takes for government deflationary policy to work

**88 Which of the following groups do NOT lose out from inflation?**

(i) Those on fixed incomes

(ii) Those who have index-linked incomes

(iii) Those who hold onto cash

(iv) Those who invest in non-financial assets

A (i) and (ii)

B (i) and (iii)

C (ii) and (iii)

D (ii) and (iv)

**89 A downturn in the level of economic activity is likely to lead to which type of unemployment?**

A seasonal

B frictional

C structural

D cyclical

**90 A reduction in the demand for coal and steel is likely to lead to which type of unemployment?**

A voluntary

B frictional

C structural

D cyclical

**91 If the government were to pursue a contractionary monetary policy they would**

A raise interest rates and sell securities

B lower interest rates and sell securities

C raise interest rates and buy securities

D lower interest rates and buy securities

**92 The major impact of an increase in the reserve asset ratio would be**

A to push up interest rates

B to reduce interest rates

C to reduce the level of liquidity in the banking sector

D to raise the level of liquidity in the banking sector

**93 The burden of an indirect tax will fall more heavily on the consumer in which of the following situations?**

A the greater is the price elasticity of demand for the good

B the lower is the price elasticity of demand for the good

C the greater is the income elasticity of demand for the good

D the lower is the price elasticity of supply

**94 If the government wishes to pursue an expansionary fiscal policy it should perform which of the following actions?**

A increase taxes, increase government expenditure

B increase taxes, reduce government expenditure

C reduce taxes, increase government expenditure

D reduce taxes, reduce government expenditure

**95 Which of the following is NOT a reason why a government should have a budget deficit?**

A political commitments

B an ageing population

C a downturn in the level of economic activity

D a fall in unemployment

**96 Which of the following statements is true?**

A Keynesian economists prefer to use fiscal policy such as changing interest rates to control the economy

B Keynesian economists prefer to use monetary policy such as changing interest rates to control the economy

C Keynesian economists prefer to use fiscal policy such as amending taxes to control the economy

D Keynesian economists prefer to use monetary policy such as amending taxes to control the economy

**97 Which of the following government policies would NOT raise the long-term rate of economic growth?**

A encouraging a higher level of business investment

B increasing expenditure on education and training

C providing tax relief for companies engaged in research and development

D trying to encourage a greater amount of consumers' expenditure

**98 When a government wishes to control inflation, it does so for which of the following reasons?**

A To redistribute wealth from rich to poor people

B Inflation damages international competitiveness

C Low Inflation increases government tax revenue

D Low inflation reduces unemployment

**99 If governments were seeking to reduce unemployment, they should perform which of the following actions?**

A reduce interest rates, raise taxes

B reduce interest rates, lower taxes

C increase interest rates, lower taxes

D increase interest rates, raise taxes

**100 Which of the following is NOT an argument in favour of a minimum wage?**

A it seeks to eliminate the poverty trap

B it seeks to prevent voluntary unemployment

C it prevents people from working below the minimum wage

D it seeks a more favourable distribution of income and wealth

**101 Which of the below is an example of fiscal policy?**

A The central bank imposing controls on commercial banks

B The removal of regulations which restrict Sunday trading

C The removal of foreign exchange controls which restrict the transfer of currencies between countries

D The creation of tax-exempt individual savings accounts

**102 A company will need to borrow money for a period of a year, with the borrowing starting in 6 months' time. The current borrowing rate offered by the company's bank is 3.5%. It has also been offered a forward rate agreement (FRA) with an interest rate of 4% and chooses to use this to hedge its borrowing rate. On the date the borrowing is made, the interest rate has moved to 5%. Which of the below is the overall rate that the company's borrowing is exposed to?**

A 3.5%

B 4%

C 5%

D 7.5%

**103 A company will lend $1 million in 3 months' time. It enters into a forward rate agreement (FRA) with a bank to guarantee a rate of 4% for this lending. In 3 months' time, the market lending rate is 3%. How much interest is transferred via the FRA and in which direction?**

A 1 to the FRA bank

B 1% from the FRA bank

C 4% to the FRA bank

D 4% from the FRA bank

# MACROECONOMIC AND INSTITUTIONAL CONTEXT II: THE INTERNATIONAL ECONOMY

**104 Which ONE of the following is NOT an economic advantage of international trade?**

A It encourages international specialisation

B Consumer choice is widened

C It enables industries to secure economies of large-scale production

D Trade surpluses can be used to finance the budget deficit

**105 Which of the following is NOT an example of protectionism?**

A Export subsidy

B Fixed exchange rate

C Import quota

D Import tariff

**106 Why do countries impose tariffs on foreign goods?**

A To prevent unemployment overseas

B To prevent unemployment at home

C To encourage free trade

D To help lesser developed countries

**107 Which of the following best describes a customs union?**

A an area of the world where you pay no tax

B an area with the same unit of currency

C a free trade area which requires fixed exchange rates between member countries

D a free trade area within a certain group of countries who have a common tariff with the rest of the world

**108 If the elasticity of demand for British exports is –2, then a devaluation of sterling should lead to**

A a fall in the value of exports

B an increase in the value of imports

C an increase in the total foreign currency expenditure on British goods

D British goods becoming more expensive overseas

**109** Consider the following figures

| | |
|---|---|
| Tangible exports | $35,432 million |
| Tangible imports | $36,607 million |
| Invisible balance | $1,429 million |
| Current account | $254 million |
| Capital account | –$2,227 million |

**The visible trade balance was:**

[ ] **million**

**110 Which one of the following will appear in the financial account of the balance of payments for Japan?**

A The export of whisky

B The purchase of Euros to go on a European holiday

C Interest received on a United States government bond

D Inflow of investment by a hi-tech multinational into Japan

**111 A balance of payments deficit is least likely to be corrected by which of the following actions?**

A imposing tariffs on imports

B increasing the value of sterling

C reducing the level of aggregate demand

D discouraging imports

**112 A tariff restriction imposed on the flow of imports into a country would be expected to lead to all of the following except which one?**

A an improvement in the trade balance

B a reduction in unemployment

C reduced competition for domestic producers

D a fall in the rate of inflation

**113 All of the following are characteristics of a common (single) market EXCEPT which ONE?**

A Free trade in goods and services among member states

B Common levels of direct taxation

C Free movement of factors of production between member states

D Common policies on product regulation

**114 If a group of countries adopt free trade themselves, establish a common external tariff and allow free movement of factors of production between member states, what is this called?**

A A single market

B An economic union

C A customs union

D A free trade area

**115 Which of the following statements is false?**

A International trade allows countries to specialise

B International trade allows consumers to a wider range of goods and services

C International trade brings about economies of scale

D International trade leads to international competition and higher prices

**116 Which TWO of the following would lead a country's balance of payments current account to move towards a surplus?**

A A rise in commodity exports

B An inflow of foreign capital into the economy

C An increase in foreign tourism into the country

D An increase in government tax receipts

**117 A deficit on a country's balance of payments current account can be financed by a surplus:**

A of exports over imports

B of invisible exports over invisible imports

C on the capital account

D of taxes over expenditure

**118 All of the following statements are true EXCEPT which ONE?**

A Import quotas tend to reduce prices

B Trade protection tends to reduce consumer choice

C Trade protection tends to reduce exports

D Tariffs tend to reduce competition

**119 Which ONE of the following is NOT associated with the process of the globalisation of production?**

A Rising trade ratios for economies

B Concentration of production close to markets

C Increasing production by transnational corporations

D Increased international factor mobility

**120 All of the following will encourage the process of the globalisation of production EXCEPT which ONE?**

A Reductions in international transport costs

B Higher levels of tariffs

C Reduced barriers to international capital movements

D Increased similarity in demand patterns between countries

**121 A sushi restaurant chain finds that demand for its food in a foreign country has increased rapidly over the past decade. This is an example of an impact of**

A internationalisation

B protectionism

C aggregation

D globalisation

**122 All of the following are features of globalisation except one. Which one is the exception?**

A rising trade ratios

B increased international capital flows

C improved terms of trade for all countries

D reduced barriers to international factor movements

**123 With reference to PESTEL analysis, which ONE of the following statements is true?**

A One form of political risk is government measures to improve the competitiveness of national companies

B Political risk is confined to less developed countries

C A tax increase is never the result of political forces and can therefore not be considered a political risk

D All of the above

**124 Which of the following would a transport company monitor under the Political heading as part of a PESTEL analysis?**

A Tracking systems to monitor driver hours/anti-theft devices/developments in tyre technology.

B State of the economy/oil price movements/a rise in interest rates.

C Fuel tax/congestion charges in cities/plans to build new roads.

D Predicted car numbers and usage/public concerns over safety.

**125 W is a national chain of bars and night clubs considering extending their operations overseas. Match up the following macro-economic factors with the heading they would be analysed under in a PESTEL analysis.**

| Political | Economic | Social | Technological | Legal | Environmental |
|---|---|---|---|---|---|

| | |
|---|---|
| The age at which people are allowed to drink alcohol | |
| Government tax on sales of alcohol | |
| The level of disposable income people have | |
| People's religious beliefs and attitudes towards alcohol | |

# FINANCIAL CONTEXT OF BUSINESS II: INTERNATIONAL ASPECTS

**126 Which ONE of the following is a characteristic of floating (flexible) exchange rates?**

A They provide automatic correction for balance of payments deficits and surpluses.

B They reduce uncertainty for businesses.

C Transactions costs involved in exchanging currencies are eliminated.

D They limit the ability of governments to adopt expansionary policies.

**127 The main advantage of a system of flexible or floating exchange rates is that it:**

A provides certainty for those engaged in international trade

B provides automatic correction of balance of payments

C reduces international transaction costs

D provides discipline for government economic management

**128** The advantages of dirty floating exchange rates include:

(i) making a country's exports more competitive

(ii) assisting in the control of inflation

**Which of these are true?**

A (i) only

B (ii) only

C both statements

D neither statement

**129 A devaluation of the exchange rate for a country's currency will normally result in which TWO of the following:**

A a reduction in the current account deficit

B an improvement in the country's terms of trade

C a reduction in the domestic cost of living

D an increased level of domestic economic activity

**130 What is the impact of a fall in the value of a country's currency?**

1 Exports will be given a stimulus

2 The rate of domestic inflation will rise

A 1 only

B 2 only

C Both 1 and 2

D Neither 1 or 2

**131 Which of the following is NOT a benefit of a single currency?**

A reduced transaction costs

B lower interest rates

C reduced exchange rate uncertainty

D increased price transparency

**132 The major disadvantage of a single currency to an individual country is:**

A loss of monetary control

B loss of fiscal control

C higher transaction costs

D none of the above

**133 Which one of the following would likely lead to a fall in the value of sterling against the dollar?**

A a rise in UK interest rates

B a rise in US interest rates

C the Bank of England buying sterling for dollars

D capital investment flows from New York to London

**134 The current rate of exchange between the UK and the United States is £1 = $1.50. The sterling price of a Jaguar car is £100,000. If the exchange rate moves to £1 = $1.40 and the sterling price remains the same, what will be the new dollar price of the car?**

| $ |
|---|

**135 Which of the following is unlikely to affect the demand for sterling?**

A An increase in UK exports

B An increase in UK imports

C Government intervention to support the exchange rate

D Overseas investors making investments in the UK

**136 A company orders a new machine from a foreign supplier with payment in the foreign currency. Unfortunately, the domestic currency weakens during the credit period resulting in the machine costing more than originally expected. This is an example of which type of foreign exchange risk?**

A Transaction risk

B Translation risk

C Economic risk

D Default risk

**137 'There is a risk that the value of our foreign currency denominated assets and liabilities will change when we prepare our accounts.' To which type of risk does this statement refer?**

A Translation risk

B Economic risk

C Transaction risk

D Interest rate risk

**138 All of the following can lead to a rise in the exchange rate (appreciation) for a country except one. Which one is the exception?**

A High inflation

B An increase in interest rates

C A trade surplus

D Speculation

**139 In comparison to forward contracts, which of the following are true in relation to futures contracts?**

(i) they are more expensive

(ii) they are only available in a small amount of currencies

(iii) they are less flexible

(iv) they are probably an imprecise match for the underlying contract

A (i), (ii) and (iv) only

B (ii) and (iv) only

C (ii) and (iii) only

D All of the above

**140** Eady plc is a UK company that imports furniture from a Canadian supplier and sells it throughout Europe. Eady plc has just received a shipment of furniture, invoiced in Canadian dollars, for which payment is to be made in two months' time. Neither Eady plc nor the Canadian supplier use hedging techniques to cover their exchange risk.

**If the pound sterling were to weaken substantially against the Canadian dollar, what would be the foreign exchange gain or loss effects upon Eady plc and the Canadian supplier? Indicate your answers by clicking in the appropriate box.**

| | Gain | Loss | No effect |
|---|---|---|---|
| Eady plc | | | |
| Canadian supplier | | | |

**141** Edted plc has to pay a Spanish supplier 100,000 euros in three months' time. The company's Finance Director wishes to avoid exchange rate exposure and is looking at four alternatives.

1 Do nothing for three months and then buy euros at the spot rate

2 Pay in full now, buying euros at today's spot rate

3 Buy euros now, put them on deposit for three months, and pay the debt with these euros plus accumulated interest

4 Arrange a forward exchange contract to buy the euros in three months' time

**Which of these alternatives would provide cover against the exchange rate exposure that Edted would otherwise suffer?**

A Option 4 only

B Options 3 and 4 only

C Options 2, 3 and 4 only

D Options 1, 2, 3 and 4

# FINANCIAL CONTEXT OF BUSINESS III: DISCOUNTING AND INVESTMENT APPRAISAL

**142 A credit card company is charging an annual percentage rate of 25.3%. This is equivalent to a monthly rate of (to one decimal place)**

[ ] %

**143** A bank offers different bank accounts with different interest rates:

- Bank account 1 = 10% flat interest per year, interest calculated quarterly
- Bank account 2 = 12% flat interest per year, interest calculated monthly
- Bank account 3 = 1.2% interest per month
- Bank account 4 = 3% interest per quarter

**Which account gives the highest annual effective interest rate?**

A 1

B 2

C 3

D 4

**144 A company is expecting an income stream of $10,000 over the next four years. If a discount rate of 10% is to be applied, the level of income in Year 4 should be worth (in today's terms).**

A $9,090

B $8,260

C $7,510

D $6,830

**145** HJF Co is considering a project which has the following cash flows:

| Timing | 0 | 1 | 2 | 3 |
|---|---|---|---|---|
| Cash flow ($000) | (200) | 750 | 500 | (300) |

**Calculate the NPV using a discount rate of 10% to the nearest $000.**

$ [ ] **,000**

**146 An annual rent of $2,000 is to be received for ten successive years with the first payment due tomorrow. The relevant rate of interest is 8%. Calculate the present value of this stream of cash flows.**

A $15,420

B $13,420

C $12,500

D $14,494

**147 A building society adds interest monthly to investors' accounts even though interest rates are expressed in annual terms. The current quoted rate of interest is 6 per cent per annum. An investor deposits $1,000 on 1 January. How much interest will have been earned by 30 June?**

A $30.00

B $30.38

C $60.00

D $61.68

**148 If LND's new investment project generates NPV of $928 when the discount rate is 10% and –$628 when the discount rate is 20%, what is the internal rate of return (to 2 decimal places)?**

[ ] %

**149 How much would FGH need to invest now at 5% to yield an annual income of $8,000 in perpetuity, starting in 1 year's time?**

A $12,000

B $140,000

C $160,000

D $200,000

**150 How much (to the nearest $10) would need to be invested today at 6% per annum to provide an annuity of $5,000 per annum for ten years commencing in five years' time?**

A $5,000

B $19,000

C $29,150

D $39,420

**151** G plc plans to borrow $50,000 with a 'mortgage style' repayment pattern where the same amount is repaid each year. This payment is a mixture of capital and interest and ensures no additional loan repayment is required at the end.

**What is the annual repayment on a bank loan of $50,000 over eight years at 9%?**

A $8,975

B $9,033

C $9,214

D $9,416

**152** JAH Company is about to invest $400,000 in machinery and other capital equipment for a new product venture. Cash flows for the first three years are estimated as follows:

| Year | $000 |
|---|---|
| 1 | 210 |
| 2 | 240 |
| 3 | 320 |

**JAH Company requires a 17% return for projects of this type. What is the NPV of this venture?**

A –$154,670

B $45,010

C $220,450

D $154,670

**153** A company has determined that the net present value of an investment project is $17,706 when using a 10% discount rate and $(4,317) when using a discount rate of 15%.

**What is the internal rate of return of the project to the nearest 1%?**

[ ] %

**154** An education authority is considering the implementation of a CCTV (closed circuit television) security system in one of its schools. Details of the proposed project are as follows:

| | |
|---|---|
| Life of project | 5 years |
| Initial cost | $75,000 |
| Annual savings: | |
| Labour costs | $20,000 |
| Other costs | $5,000 |
| NPV at 15% | $8,800 |

**What is the internal rate of return for this project (use 25% as the second discount rate) to the nearest whole percent?**

[ ] %

**155** **A landlord receives a rent of $1,000 to be received over ten successive years. The first payment is due now. If interest rates are 8%, what is the present value of this income?**

A $6,951

B $7,345

C $7,247

D $8,138

**156** **What is the main reason that NPV techniques are used to determine the impact of shareholder wealth of different projects?**

A The increase in profit attributable to the shareholders is clearly shown

B Shareholders are interested in cash, not profit

C The directors can decide how much additional salary to pay themselves

D The technique is easy to use as the time value of money is ignored

**157** An amount of $65,000 is invested today to provide an annuity income for the next ten years, starting in 1 year.

**If the interest rate is 7%, what, to the nearest $10, will be the annual cash value of the annuity income?**

A $13,350

B $11,120

C $9,940

D $9,250

**158** Gerber is undertaking a project which has a net present value of $(543) when the discount rate is 20 per cent and $3,802 when it is 15 per cent.

**Which of the following statements about the value of the internal rate of return (IRR) is correct in this case?**

A The IRR must be below 10 per cent

B The IRR must lie between 10 per cent and 15 per cent

C The IRR must lie between 15 per cent and 20 per cent

D The IRR much be greater than 20 per cent

**159** CC Company is considering an investment of $300,000 which will earn a contribution of $40,000 each year for 10 years at today's prices, starting in 1 year's time. The company's cost of capital is 11% per annum.

**What is the net present value of the project?**

A $(64,440)

B $23,556

C $64,440

D $235,560

**160** Consider the following graph.

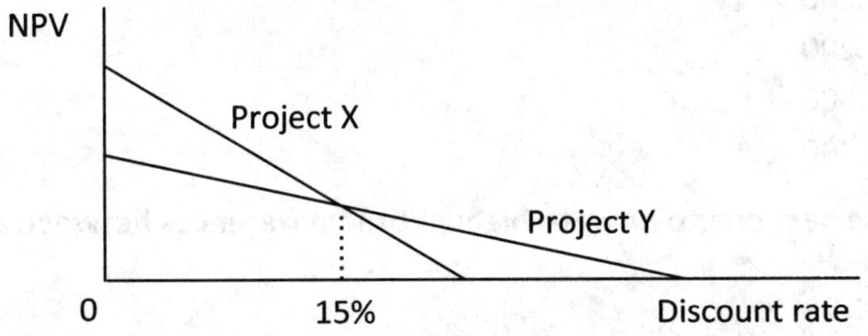


**Which TWO statements are true?**

A Project Y has a higher internal rate of return than project X

B At discount rates of less than 15%, project X is preferred to project Y

C Project X is preferred to project Y irrespective of discount rate

D Project Y is preferred to project X irrespective of discount rate

**161** Investment is possible in one or more of three projects.

| | A | B | C |
|---|---|---|---|
| | $ | $ | $ |
| Outlay | 10,000 | 7,000 | 1,250 |
| Expected returns ($t_1 - t_4$) | 4,000 | 2,500 | 325 |

The firm can borrow the finance at 10% pa.

**Which project(s) should be undertaken?**

A A only

B A and B

C A and C

D A and B and C

# INFORMATIONAL CONTEXT OF BUSINESS I: SUMMARISING AND ANALYSING DATA

**162 Which of the following graphs would best be used to illustrate that two variables are uncorrelated?**

A A bar chart

B A pie chart

C A line graph

D A scatter graph

**163** The following table shows that the typical salary of part qualified accountants in five different regions of a country.

| Area | Typical salary |
|---|---|
| | $ |
| South-east | 21,500 |
| Midlands | 20,800 |
| North-east | 18,200 |
| North-west | 17,500 |
| South-west | 16,700 |

**Which diagram would be the best one to draw to highlight the differences between areas?**

A a pie diagram

B a multiple bar chart

C a percentage component bar chart

D a simple bar chart

**164 A scatter graph is being produced to show the cost of advertising and sales revenue for a business. Which values would be shown on which axis?**

A Both on the y-axis

B Both on the x-axis

C Cost of advertising on the x-axis and sales revenue on the y-axis

D Sales revenue on the x-axis and cost of advertising on the y-axis

**165 XYZ produces three main products. Which would be the most appropriate chart or diagram for showing total revenue analysed into product revenue month by month?**

A Scatter graph

B Line graph

C Pie chart

D Component bar chart

**166 Cumulative frequencies in an ogive are plotted against**

A the mid-point

B the lower class boundaries

C the upper class boundaries

D any of the above

**167 Which member of the sales team had the highest sales in February?**

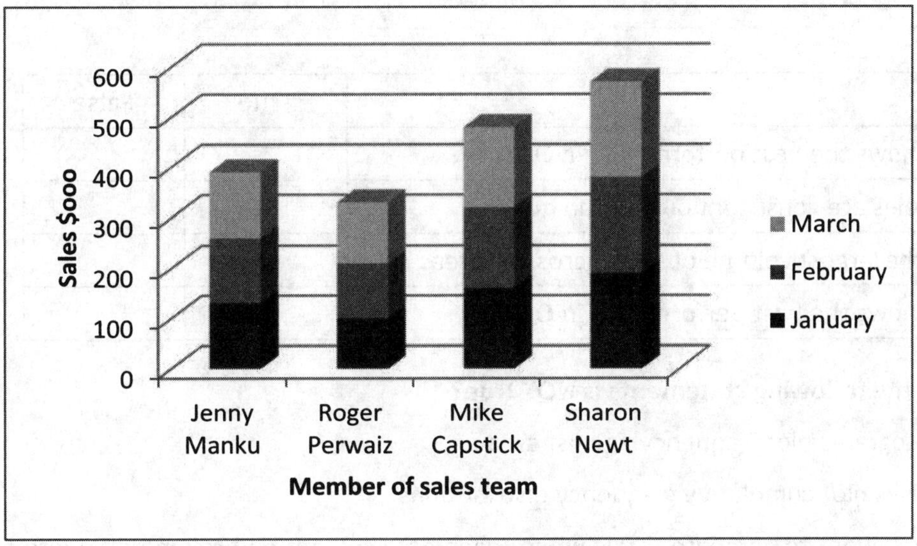


A Jenny Manku

B Roger Perwaiz

C Mike Capstick

D Sharon Newt

**168 A histogram uses a set of rectangles to represent a grouped frequency table. To be correctly represented, the histogram must show the relationship of the rectangles to the frequencies by reference to which of the following?**

A Height of each rectangle

B Area of each rectangle

C Width of each rectangle

D Diagonal of each rectangle

**169 Referring to the graph which statements are true and which are false?**

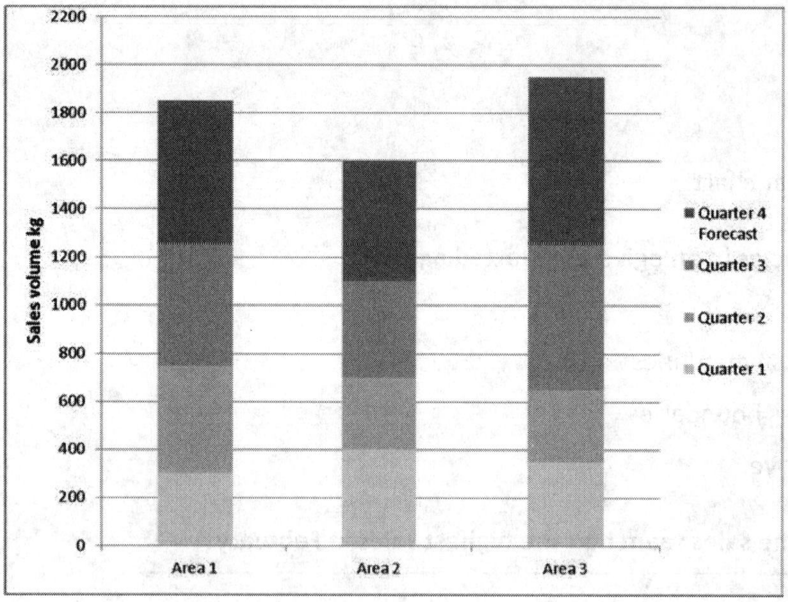


| | True | False |
|---|---|---|
| Area 3 shows the best performance in Q3 | | |
| Area 2 sales are consistent quarter on quarter | | |
| Q4 has the largest volume of sales across all areas | | |
| Area 1 shows the best performance in Q2 | | |

**170 Which of the following statements is NOT true?**

A Histograms plot frequency against area

B Ogives plot cumulative frequency distributions

C If you want to compare totals where each data set can be broken down into further data sets, a compound bar chart would be more useful than a multiple bar chart

D Scatter diagrams plot a dependent variable against an independent variable

**171** A frequency distribution of a sample of monthly incomes is as follows:

| $ | Frequency |
|---|---|
| 400 and less than 800 | 7 |
| 800 and less than 1,000 | 16 |
| 1,000 and less than 1,200 | 28 |
| 1,200 and less than 1,300 | 21 |
| 1,300 and less than 1,400 | 8 |
| | 80 |

**If the rectangle representing incomes between $800 to less than $1,000 has a height of 8 cm, what is the height of the rectangle $1,000 and less than $1,200?**

[ ] **cm**

**172 Which of the following qualities is NOT necessarily a quality of good information?**

A It should be relevant

B It should be understandable

C It should be worth more than it costs to produce

D It should be available quickly

**173 Which of the following is correct?**

A Qualitative data is generally non-numerical information

B Information can only be extracted from external sources

C Operational information gives details of long-term plans only

D Quantitative data is always accurate

**174 Which of the following would be classified as data?**

A Number of purchase requisitions

B Analysis of wages into direct and indirect costs

C Table showing variances from budget

D Graph showing the number of labour hours worked

**175 Which of the following statements is/are true regarding the qualities of good information? Indicate your answer by ticking in the appropriate box.**

| | **True** | **False** |
|---|---|---|
| It should be communicated to the right person | | |
| It should always be completely accurate before it is used | | |
| It should be understandable by the recipient | | |

**176 Which of the following only contains essential features of useful management information?**

A Accurate, understandable, presented in report format

B Timely, reliable, supported by calculations

C Regular, complete, communicated in writing

D Understandable, accurate, relevant for its purpose

**177 Which of the following describes 'Information'?**

A data that consists of facts and statistics before they have been processed.

B data that consists of numbers, letters, symbols, events and transactions which have been recorded but not yet processed into a form that is suitable for making decisions.

C facts that have been summarised but not yet processed into a form that is suitable for making decisions.

D data that has been processed in such a way that it has a meaning to the person who receives it, who may then use it to improve the quality of decision making.

**178 Which TWO of the following statements relating to Big Data are true?**

A Big Data refers to any financial data over $1 billion

B Managing Big Data effectively can lead to increased competitive advantage

C The term Big Data means 'data that comes from many sources'

D Big Data contains both financial and non-financial data

**179 Which THREE of the following are typical problems that organisations may face when dealing with Big Data?**

A The increasing use of electronic devices within society at large

B A lack of skills in the labour pool relating to the handling of Big Data

C Legal and privacy issues if data is held about individuals

D Measurement of metrics that have no use to the organisation

E Inability to monitor information from social media sites

# MACROECONOMIC AND INSTITUTIONAL CONTEXT III: INDEX NUMBERS

**180 If an index of average gross earning with base year 2011 and at constant 2011 prices is calculated to be 107 by 2016, which of the following statements is correct about changes in average gross earnings over this 5-year period?**

A A total of 1.07 per cent more goods and services can be bought by average earnings

B A total of 7 per cent more goods and services can be bought by average earnings

C Earnings have risen by 1.07 per cent

D The average price of goods and services has risen by 7 per cent

**181 In which of the following ways could a price index of 235 be interpreted?**

(i) There has been a 35 per cent increase since the base year

(ii) There has been a 135 per cent increase since the base year

(iii) There has been a 235 per cent increase since the base year

(iv) Prices now are 2.35 times what they were in the base year

A (i) only

B (ii) only

C (ii) and (iv) only

D (iii) and (iv) only

**182** An inflation index and index numbers of a company's sales ($) for the last year are given below.

| Quarter | 1 | 2 | 3 | 4 |
|---|---|---|---|---|
| Sales ($) index | 109 | 120 | 132 | 145 |
| Inflation index | 100 | 110 | 121 | 133 |

**Which of the following statements is true? 'Real' sales, i.e. adjusted for inflation, are:**

A approximately constant and keeping up with inflation

B growing steadily and not keeping up with inflation

C growing steadily and keeping ahead of inflation

D falling steadily and not keeping up with inflation

**183** Details of an index number are given below.

| Group | Base | Weight | Index |
|---|---|---|---|
| Food and drink | 100 | 50 | 140 |
| Travel and Leisure | 100 | 30 | 130 |
| Housing | 100 | 20 | 120 |
| All items | 100 | 100 | ? |

Calculate the 'All items' weighted index number,

[ ]

**184** A weighted average index number is made up of two items, food and non-food.

| Sub-group | Weight | Index |
|---|---|---|
| Non-food | 7 | 130 |
| Food | 3 | ? |
| All items | 10 | 127 |

**The index number for the sub-group Food is closest to which of the following?**

A 120

B 122

C 124

D 126

**185 The price index for a commodity in the current year is 87 (base year = 100) and the current price is $490 per unit. What was the price in the base year, to the nearest cent?**

[ $ ]

**186 If a price index is 102, which TWO of the following statements are correct about average prices?**

A Prices have risen by 102 per cent since the base year

B Prices are now 1.02 times their base year value

C Prices have risen by 2 per cent since the base year

D Prices have risen by 98 per cent since the base year

**187 Magnetise uses material X in their production process daily. Two years ago the price index appropriate to the cost of material X had a value of 120. It now has a value of 160. If material X costs $2,000/kg today, what would its cost/kg have been two years ago?**

A $1,500

B $1,667

C $2,667

D $3,200

**188** A business wishes to calculate an index in relation to the following data:

| | Price this year ($) | Price last year ($) | Quantity sold this year | Quantity sold last year |
|---|---|---|---|---|
| Bread | 1.50 | 1.20 | 1,000 | 800 |
| Milk | 0.90 | 0.60 | 5,000 | 4,000 |
| Biscuits | 1.10 | 1.00 | 1,500 | 750 |

**What is the base weighted relative price index using quantities as the weighting?**

A 110.0

B 125.0

C 128.3

D 141.0

**189** A business wishes to calculate an index in relation to the following data:

| | Price this year ($) | Price last year ($) | Quantity sold this year | Quantity sold last year |
|---|---|---|---|---|
| Bread | 1.50 | 1.20 | 1,000 | 800 |
| Milk | 0.90 | 0.60 | 5,000 | 4,000 |
| Biscuits | 1.10 | 1.00 | 1,500 | 750 |

**What is the base weighted relative quantity index using prices as the weighting, to 1 decimal place?**

[ ]

**190** A business wishes to calculate an index in relation to the following data:

| | Price this year ($) | Price last year ($) | Quantity sold this year | Quantity sold last year |
|---|---|---|---|---|
| Bread | 1.50 | 1.20 | 1,000 | 800 |
| Milk | 0.90 | 0.60 | 5,000 | 4,000 |
| Biscuits | 1.10 | 1.00 | 1,500 | 750 |

**What is the current weighted relative price index using quantities as the weighting?**

A 125.0

B 138.7

C 141.0

D 150.0

**191** A business wishes to calculate an index in relation to the following data:

| | Price this year ($) | Price last year ($) | Quantity sold this year | Quantity sold last year |
|---|---|---|---|---|
| Bread | 1.50 | 1.20 | 1,000 | 800 |
| Milk | 0.90 | 0.60 | 5,000 | 4,000 |
| Biscuits | 1.10 | 1.00 | 1,500 | 750 |

**What is the current weighted relative quantity index using prices as the weighting, to 1 decimal place?**

[ ]

# INFORMATIONAL CONTEXT OF BUSINESS II: INTER-RELATIONSHIPS BETWEEN VARIABLES

**192** Briggs Co is seeking to establish a relationship between money spent on a dedicated customer care department and the feedback scores achieved as part of customer surveys and has decided to use linear regression with the following results.

- 'x' = spend in $000s and 'y' = score achieved (measured between –10 and +10)
- $\Sigma x = 560$, $\Sigma y = 85$, $\Sigma x^2 = 62{,}500$, $\Sigma xy = 14{,}200$ and $n = 12$.

**What is the regression line of y in relation to x?**

A $y = -0.281 + 6.03x$

B $y = -6.03 + 0.281x$

C $y = 0.281 + 6.03x$

D $y = 6.03 + 0.281x$

**193** A company uses regression analysis to establish its selling overhead costs for budgeting purposes. The data used for the analysis is as follows:

| Month | Number of salesmen | Sales overhead costs |
|---|---|---|
| 1 | 3 | 35,100 |
| 2 | 6 | 46,400 |
| 3 | 4 | 27,000 |
| 4 | 3 | 33,500 |
| 5 | 5 | 41,000 |
| | 21 | 183,000 |

**The gradient of the regression line is 4,200. Using regression analysis, what would be the budgeted sales overhead costs for the month, in $000, if there are 2 salesmen employed?**

A 27,360

B 39,960

C 41,000

D 56,760

**194** An organisation is using linear regression analysis to establish an equation that shows a relationship between advertising expenditure and sales revenue. It will then use the equation to predict sales revenue for given levels of advertising expenditure. Data for the last five periods are as follows:

| Period number | Advertising expenditure $ | Sales revenue $ |
|---|---|---|
| 1 | 17,000 | 108,000 |
| 2 | 19,000 | 116,000 |
| 3 | 24,000 | 141,000 |
| 4 | 22,000 | 123,000 |
| 5 | 18,000 | 112,000 |

**What are the values of 'Σx', 'Σy' and 'n' that need to be inserted into the appropriate formula?**

| | Σx | Σy | n |
|---|---|---|---|
| A | $600,000 | $100,000 | 5 |
| B | $100,000 | $600,000 | 5 |
| C | $600,000 | $100,000 | 10 |
| D | $100,000 | $600,000 | 10 |

**195** Over a period of 10 months a factory's monthly production costs (Y, $000) range from 5 to 16 whilst output (X, units) ranges from 50 to 500.

**If the regression equation is Y = 5.0913 + 0.2119X, which THREE of the following statements are correct?**

A When X increases by 1, Y increases by 0.2119

B Fixed costs are $5.0913

C When X = 0, Y = 5.11249

D Fixed costs are $5.091.3

E Fixed costs are $211.9

F Variable cost is $211.9 per unit

G Variable cost is $5.0913 per unit

**196 If the regression equation (in $000) linking sales (Y) to advertising expenditure (X) is given by Y = 4,000 + 12X, what is the forecast sales when $150,000 is spent on advertising, to the nearest $?**

| $ |
|---|

**197** Having analysed the data from a thousand customer loyalty cards, F plc believes it has found a link between how much is typically spent annually on average on Product X (x-variable) and how much is spent on product Y by the same customer (y variable).

The correlation coefficient for a thousand pairs of x- and y-values, with x ranging from $500 to $700, is calculated to be 0.79 and the regression equation is y = 620 + 4.3x.

**Which TWO of the following statements are correct?**

A When x = $600, the estimate of y = $3,200

B When x = $550, the estimate of y from the regression equation is likely to be reliable

C When x = 0, the estimate of y from the regression equation is likely to be reliable

D When x increases by $1, y increases by $0.79

E 79% of the differences in money spent on product Y can be explained by looking at differences in the spend on product X

**198 If there is a perfect positive correlation between two variables then the value of r, the correlation coefficient, is**

A greater than 1

B equal to 1

C equal to 0

D equal to –1

**199** The correlation coefficient (r) for measuring the connection between two variables (x and y) has been calculated as 0.6.

**How much of the variation in the dependent variable (y) is explained by the variation in the independent variable (x)?**

A 36%

B 40%

C 60%

D 64%

**200 The coefficient of determination ($r^2$) explains the**

A percentage variation in the coefficient of correlation

B percentage variation in the dependent variable which is explained by the independent variable

C percentage variation in the independent variable which is explained by the dependent variable

D extent of the casual relationship between the two variables

**201** C plc is looking to understand buying behaviour for two of its main customers – X and Y. The following table shows the ranking of six of C plc's products by the two major customers.

| Product | Customer X | Customer Y |
|---|---|---|
| A | 4 | 2 |
| B | 5 | 3 |
| C | 2 | 1 |
| D | 1 | 4 |
| E | 3 | 5 |
| F | 6 | 6 |

**What is the correlation between the behaviour of the two customers?**

A 0.31

B 0.33

C 0.35

D 0.37

**202** B plc is trying to assess the extent to which its customers perceive its more expensive products as being better. Towards this it has asked customers to rank products by quality and it has then compared this to the ranking by price.

**If data comprising 10 pairs of corresponding ranks has $\sum d^2 = 304.5$ where d represents the difference between corresponding ranks, what is Spearman's rank correlation coefficient, giving your answer correct to two decimal places?**

| |
|---|
| |

**203** A plc is assessing the impact of advertising on customer perceived quality of its products.

**If the rank correlation coefficient between variables X (advertising spend) and Y (customer perceived quality) is 0.85, which TWO of the following comments are correct?**

A Values of Y increase as values of X increase

B Y decreases by 0.15 for every increase of 1 in X

C Y increases by 0.85 for every increase of 1 in X

D The link between X and Y values is very strong

E The link between X and Y values is linear

F Increases in X cause corresponding increases in Y

# INFORMATIONAL CONTEXT OF BUSINESS III: FORECASTING

**204 Unemployment numbers actually recorded in a town for the second quarter of 2015 were 2,200. The underlying trend at this point was 2,000 people and the seasonal factor is 0.97. Using the multiplicative model for seasonal adjustment, the seasonally adjusted figure (in whole numbers) for the quarter is which of the following?**

A 1,940

B 2,061

C 2,134

D 2,268

**205 If takings at Mr Li's takeaway for the first quarter of 2015 were $25,000. The underlying trend at this point was $23,000 takings and the seasonal factor is 0.78. Assuming a multiplicative model for seasonal adjustment, what is the seasonally-adjusted figure for that quarter?**

A $19,500

B $20,500

C $32,051

D $34,051

206 In a time series analysis the multiplicative model is used to forecast sales and the following seasonal variations apply:

| 2010 | 2011 | 2012 | 2013 | 2014 | 2015 |
|---|---|---|---|---|---|
| 100 | 105 | 115 | 127 | 140 | 152 |

**It has been decided to rebase the index so that 2013 = 100. The index for 2015 will now be nearest to which of the following figures?**

A 193.1

B 139.4

C 125.0

D 119.7

**207 Over an 18 month period, sales of Parrot's best-selling product have been found to have an underlying linear trend of y = 7.112 + 3.949x where y is the number of items sold and x represents the month. Monthly deviations from trend have been calculated and month 19 is expected to be 1.12 times the trend value. What is the forecast number of items to be sold in month 19?**

A 88

B 90

C 92

D 94

**208** In data with a 4-year cycle, the cyclical components using the additive model are given to be:

| Year 1 | Year 2 | Year 3 | Year 4 |
|---|---|---|---|
| 10 | 15 | 25 | 220 |

**If 2015 is year 1 of the cycle and if the trend for 2019 is predicted to be 70, what is the predicted actual value for 2019?**

| |
|---|
| |

**209** H is forecasting its sales for next year using a combination of time series and regression analysis models. An analysis of past sales units has produced the following equation for the quarterly sales trend:

y = 26x + 8,850

where the value of x represents the quarterly accounting period and the value of y represents the quarterly sales trend in units. Quarter 1 of next year will have a value for x of 25.

The quarterly seasonal variations have been measured using the multiplicative (proportional) model and are:

| | |
|---|---|
| Quarter 1 | – 15% |
| Quarter 2 | – 5% |
| Quarter 3 | + 5% |
| Quarter 4 | + 15% |

Production is planned to occur at a constant rate throughout the year.

The company does not hold inventories at the end of any year.

**The difference between the budgeted sales for quarter 1 and quarter 4 next year are:**

A 78 units

B 2,850 units

C 2,862 units

D 2,940 units

**210** The overhead costs of RP have been found to be accurately represented by the formula:

y = $10,000 + $0.25x

where 'y' is the monthly cost and 'x' represents the activity level measured as the number of orders.

Monthly activity levels of orders may be estimated using a combined regression analysis and time series model:

a = 100,000 + 30b

where 'a' represents the de-seasonalised monthly activity level (i.e. the trend) and 'b' represents the month number.

In month 240, the seasonal index value is 108.

**The overhead cost for RP for month 240 is $____________ (round to the nearest $1,000)**

**211** Monthly sales of product R follow a linear trend of y = 9.72 + 5.816x, where y is the number of units sold and x is the number of the month. Monthly deviations from the trend follow an additive model.

**The forecast number of units of product R to be sold in month 23, which has a seasonal factor of plus 6.5 is, to the nearest whole unit:**

A 134

B 137

C 143

D 150

**212** Z plc has found that it can estimate future sales using time series analysis and regression techniques. The following trend equation has been derived:

y = 25,000 + 6,500x

where

y is the total sales units per quarter

x is the time period reference number

Z has also derived the following set of seasonal variation index values for each quarter using a multiplicative (proportional) model:

| | |
|---|---|
| Quarter 1 | 70 |
| Quarter 2 | 90 |
| Quarter 3 | 150 |
| Quarter 4 | 90 |

**Assuming that the first quarter of year 1 is time period reference number 1, the forecast for sales units for the third quarter of year 7, is ____________ units.**

Section 2

# ANSWERS TO OBJECTIVE TEST QUESTIONS

## MICROECONOMIC AND ORGANISATIONAL CONTEXT I: THE GOALS AND DECISIONS OF ORGANISATIONS

**1 D**

Organisations do not have to create a product or service in order to be classified as an organisation. For example, an orchestra may be classed as an organisation, but it does not necessarily create a product.

**2 C**

C is the correct answer because this is the main activity in the public sector. Options A and B relate to the private sector and D to a mutual organisation.

**3 C**

Not-for-profit organisations can be found in both sectors, for example private sector charity and public sector local authority.

**4 B**

Partnerships and companies would both usually be profit seeking. While government departments are likely to be not-for-profit, they would be part of the public sector. Therefore, only charities would be likely to be both private AND not-for-profit.

**5 A**

NFPs may have radically different objectives – a charity may aim to help, say, animals under threat of extinction while a hospital may wish to treat its patients as effectively as possible.

Government funded organisations are usually concerned with providing basic government services. This does not always involve minimising the costs of their operations.

**6** An example of the principal-agent problem in business is where principals, such as **shareholders**, delegate control to agents, such as management. The problem is one of devising methods to ensure that agents act in the best interest of the principals. Managerial reward systems which link pay and bonuses to the improvement in **shareholder wealth** is one such method.

Directors make decisions on behalf of the shareholders.

**7 $0.08**

EPS = profit after interest, tax and preference share dividends/number of shares issued.

= ($110,000 – $45,000 – $30,000 – $15,000)/($125,000/$0.5)

= $20,000/250,000 = $0.08 per share

**8 C**

$$\frac{8.6}{204} \times 100 = 4.2\%$$

**9 D**

PAT will already include a deduction for interest paid.

$$\text{EPS} = \frac{\$17,000}{70,000} = \$0.243 \text{ per share}$$

**10 A**

A is the correct answer because this measure shows that the company is maximising short-run profit in relation to assets to increase shareholder wealth. Net present value is related to investment, which measures long run increases in shareholder wealth.

**11 C**

C is the correct answer because shareholder wealth is determined more by long-term cash flows than short-term earnings.

**12 C**

C is the correct answer because this relates to an increase in shareholder wealth in the long run. The other measures are relevant when measuring short-run shareholder value.

**13 A**

Internal includes employees and managers/directors; connected includes shareholders, customers, suppliers, and finance providers. The third stakeholder group is external which includes the community at large, government and trade unions.

**14 A and C**

Connected stakeholders either invest in or have dealings with FCC.

B and D are internal stakeholders, while E and F are external stakeholders.

**15 C**

C is the correct answer because other options normally erode shareholder value; maximising cash flows improves shareholder value.

**16 A**

A is the correct answer because, although improving employee welfare is important, this is not seen as a primary objective of corporate governance.

**17 Statement 1: True Statement 2: False**

Statement 1: True is the correct answer because good governance enables companies to improve their credit ratings, thus improving access to forms of capital.

Statement 2: False is the correct answer because these roles are normally split to avoid too much power being given to one person.

**18 C**

When outsourcing, transaction costs arise from the effort that must be put into specifying what is required and subsequently co-ordinating delivery and monitoring quality.

# MICROECONOMIC AND ORGANISATIONAL CONTEXT II: THE MARKET SYSTEM

**19 –1.25**

Elasticity of demand, non-average arc method

$$= \frac{\text{\% change in quantity demanded, based on original quantity}}{\text{\% change in price, based on original price}} = \frac{+25\%}{-20\%} = -1.25$$

**20 –1**

Elasticity of demand

$$= \frac{\text{\% change in quantity demanded, based on average quantity}}{\text{\% change in price, based on average price}} = \frac{+22.22\%}{-22.22\%} = -1$$

**21 D**

The price of the good itself is not held constant when we draw the demand curve.

**22 B**

B is the correct answer because demand measures the quantity of a product that consumers will purchase at different price levels. Only the price of the product is allowed to vary to construct a demand curve.

**23 C**

C is the correct answer because it shows a movement along a demand curve; supply is unaffected (in fact no supply curve is shown).

**24 B**

B is the correct answer because raising prices usually causes fewer people to demand the product – a contraction in demand.

**25 D**

D is the correct answer because this is the definition of a complementary good.

**26** The correct completed sentences are:

If the price of a good rises, there will be a contraction along the demand curve.

If disposable income increases, there will be a shift to the right of the demand curve.

If the supply of the good increases there will be an expansion along the demand curve (and a lowering of price, reaching the new equilibrium point of supply and demand).

If the price of a substitute falls, there will be a shift to the left of the demand curve.

**27 D**

A and B refer to the supply curve.

C causes a movement along the Demand curve.

An increase in demand for the complementary good would create an increase in demand for this product at all price levels (a shift to the right).

**28 D**

D is the correct answer because technological progress increases the efficiency of production and lowers costs, meaning that suppliers would be willing to produce more for the same price.

A would cause an expansion along the curve. B and C have the opposite effect to D, increasing costs and causing a shift to the left.

**29 B and C**

With elastic products, the change in demand is proportionally higher than the change in price, so raising its price will reduce demand by a proportionally higher figure and revenue will fall. Lowering the price will increase demand by a higher proportion and increase the revenue earned. For inelastic products, the opposite is true.

**30 D**

Habit affects the price elasticity of demand rather than supply.

**31 B**

A government subsidy, an increase in technology and lower input prices would all shift the supply curve to the right, a government expenditure tax would shift to the left.

**32 D**

$$\text{Elasticity of supply} = \frac{\text{\% change in quantity supplied, based on original quantity}}{\text{\% change in price, based on original price}} = \frac{+20\%}{+10\%} = +2$$

**33 C**

The supply of agricultural products in the short run is inelastic. To amend supply needs planning well in advance to, for example, amend which crop is grown in a particular field. Therefore, supply will not change much in the short run after a price change.

**34 A**

This will lead to excess demand. Suppliers can't charge as much as customers would be willing to pay. Suppliers won't be willing to supply as much at this price as at the equilibrium price, but customers would be willing to purchase more at this lower price than at the equilibrium one.

**35 B and C**

To increase supply quickly, the industry must have spare capacity to do so. If a product has a long lead time then, even if production commences immediately, it may not get to market for a long time. If import tariffs are high then the supply increase is unlikely to come from abroad and so the increase is dependent on domestic producers increasing their production, which could take much longer than if imports could be immediately purchased. Whether the product is a necessity or not is not relevant.

**36 D**

D is the correct answer because there is currently excess supply in the market; customers must be encouraged to purchase more of the good. The supplier needs to attract more demand – this can be done by decreasing price.

**37 B**

B is the correct answer because an increase in income will result in an overall increase in demand at all price levels. This means that the demand curve will shift to the right. The supply curve is unaffected and so the new equilibrium price has moved to point X.

**38 D**

D is the correct answer because manufacturing/supply becomes more efficient, thus moving the supply curve to the right. The demand curve is unaffected and so the new equilibrium price will be at point Z.

**39 B**

B is the correct answer because the cost of supply will increase, moving the supply curve to the left. Demand is unchanged and so the new equilibrium price will be at point W.

**40 B**

Higher elasticity is seen when customers find it easier to switch from a product to an alternative. This can occur when there are many substitutes that are easy for customers to find, with little differentiation between them.

Lower prices are not a cause of higher price elasticity in any market. They are more likely to be the effect.

**41 D**

D is the correct answer because the lead time to amend the supply of wheat in response to changes in prices is dependent on the ability to repurpose a field, plant the crop and wait for harvest time, which could be a year or more.

**42 A**

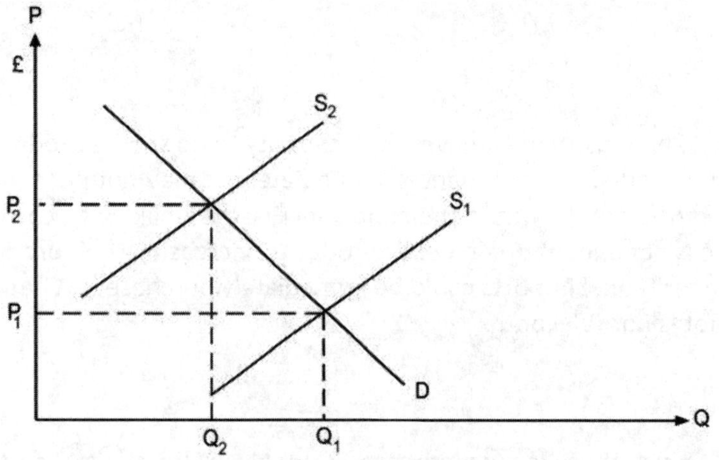


A decrease in supply means the supply curve moves to the left ($S_1$ to $S_2$). The demand curve itself would be unchanged and so the equilibrium position would move to show prices at $P_2$ instead of $P_1$ and amount sold at $Q_2$ instead of $Q_1$.

**43 D**

If a firm is enjoying economies of scale, then unit cost is falling as output rises.

**44 B**

Having workers that specialise means that they focus on a specific task or series of tasks. Productivity may be raised, as workers will become very efficient, leading to time savings. However, specialisation can lead to boredom at doing repetitive work. Economies of scale are a long run phenomenon related to size. Product differentiation is determined by company strategy rather than the type of labour force employed.

**45 A**

External economies of scale are where advantages accrue to all of the firms in an industry or area. For instance, when firms in the same industry operate in the same area, there will be a tendency for workers with the relevant skills for the industry moving to the area, reducing the level of training needed for all local businesses in the industry. B, C and D are examples of internal economies of scale (economics of scale that accrue to the firm because the firm itself gets bigger).

**46 C**

(iii) is an internal economy of scale, which accrues to specific firms due to their size.

**47 B**

A is not true, any firm can benefit from economies of scale providing they are of sufficient size to obtain such economies. C is not true by definition. D is not true. Management can generally be inefficient and still make some good decisions.

**48 D**

Health and education are examples of merit goods since they are available to the consumer below market price. Road congestion is an example of a social cost.

**49 A**

By definition

**50 A**

A pure public good is one that no individual can be excluded from consuming.

**51 A**

If a chemical company has reduced the level of pollution from its factory, this will lead to a fall in social costs (those met by society as a whole rather than the producer or consumer).

**52 B and C**

Health and education are examples of merit goods, where external social benefits accrue from their use. Defence is a public good and water is a necessity.

**53 B**

Privatisation will lead to a less even distribution of income and wealth. Firms previously owned by the state are now in the hands of comparatively few investors.

**54 D**

For example, bread is a necessity consumed by everyone, but it is not produced by the state.

**55 A**

When privatisation takes place, assets are transferred from the public sector and money goes to the government.

**56 A**

Positive externalities have social benefits rather than costs. If the production of a good results in a positive externality, the government should therefore give the producer a subsidy that reflects the marginal benefit from the consumption of the good. This increases production and the level of social benefits seen. Taxing the producer would reduce production and reduce the social benefits seen.

**57 C**

The government may discourage horizontal mergers in manufacturing industry because consumers may lose out if the merged firm acquires market dominance.

**58 D**

D is the correct answer because this action will not help producers determine how much of the good to supply.

**59 B**

The MMC had as its main brief to protect the public interest, anti-competitive behaviour would be regarded as against the public interest.

A merger should have been prevented by the Monopolies and Mergers Commission if it was not considered to be in the public interest. If the merger were to result in a monopoly situation where competition is reduced and prices rise, this would be against the public interest.

**60 B**

Governments act in the interest of consumers. They do not want to see either choice limited or prices rise.

**61 A**

Price elasticity of demand (PED) = % change in demand / % change in price.

-1.5 = % change in demand / +10

-1.5 × 10 = % change in demand = -15

If the price rises by 10%, demand will fall by 15%. 15% of current demand is (1,000 × 15%) 150 units.

1,000 – 150 = 850 units.

**62 23,727**

Price elasticity of demand (PED) = % change in demand / % change in price.

-0.8 = % change in demand / -8

-0.8 × -8 = % change in demand = +6.4

If the price falls by 8%, demand will rise by 6.4%. 6.4% of current demand is (22,300 × 6.4%) 1,427 units (to the nearest whole unit).

22,300 + 1,427 = 23,727 units.

**63 $47.50**

Price elasticity of demand (PED) = % change in demand / % change in price.

% change in demand = (50,000 – 40,000) / 40,000 × 100 = +25%

-1.2 = +25 / % change in price

% change in price = +25 / -1.2 = -20.83%

To achieve an increase of demand of 25%, the price should be lowered by 20.83%.

$60 × 20.83% = $12.498

New price = $60 – $12.498 = $47.502, or $47.50 to the nearest cent

**64 C**

Price elasticity of supply (PES) = % change in supply / % change in price.

+1.4 = % change in supply / +5

+1.4 × 5 = % change in supply = +7

If the sales price rises by 5%, the company will aim to supply 7% more units than before.

New units supplied = 12,000 × 1.07 = 12,840 units.

# FINANCIAL CONTEXT OF BUSINESS I

**65 Both statements are true** (statement 1 examples are bonds and certificates of deposit)

**66 A, B and C**

Statement 4 relates to capital markets.

**67 C**

Money markets focus on short term financial instruments. A corporate bond is a long-term source of finance, hence is a capital market instrument.

**68 A**

When a company issues shares, it uses the stock market as a primary market. As soon as the recipients of those shares start to trade them to other investors, they are using the market as a secondary market.

**69 A, C and D**

Certificates of deposits are fully negotiable and hence attractive to the depositor since they ensure instant liquidity if required.

**70 B**

Share prices are likely to fall because an increase in interest will raise borrowing costs, which will affect profit.

**71 B**

If the central bank pursues an expansionary open market operations policy it will buy securities from the public who will in turn hold the money with the banking sector, thus increasing the liquidity of the banking sector.

**72 C**

A customer's deposit account is an asset of the customer so is a liability to a clearing bank.

**73 D**

$$\text{Credit multiplier} = \frac{1}{\text{reserve asset ratio}} = \frac{1}{0.25} = 4$$

4 × \$100 = \$400

**74 A**

If the market rate of interest falls, the price of bonds will rise because they become a more attractive investment in relation to others.

**75 D**

D is the correct answer because this relates to the time period over which money is lent or borrowed.

**76 B**

B is the correct answer because the costs of finding borrowers/lenders with corresponding requirements can be high.

**77 C**

C is the correct answer because the money market has instruments maturing in less than one year while capital markets have instruments maturing in more than one year.

**78 D**

You can buy and sell shares through the Stock Exchange, but they do not actually engage in the market themselves.

**79 D**

Shares do carry higher risk relative to bonds issued by the same company as the investor has no guarantee of dividends being received and is last in line for pay-out if the company enters liquidation. Dividends are paid at the discretion of the company rather than the shareholder. Unquoted company shares are less liquid that quoted ones, as there is no organised market to trade them on. Companies may choose to redeem (buy back) shares, but it is rare and not done at the discretion of the investor (shareholder).

**80 A**

Providing finance for countries with a balance of payments deficit is not a function of GATT.

**81 D**

Yield = interest / bond price × 100

We can use this to answer the question. If the bond is to yield 5%, and its current market price is $100, then it must pay out annual interest of $5.

5% = $5 / $100 × 100

If the market rate of interest (such as on deposit accounts) falls to only 2%, investors will switch to these bonds as they offer a higher yield. But in doing so, because demand for these bonds increases, so will the price. We can work out the price to which the bonds will move by working out the price that would give the same yield as the market rate. Once the bonds get to this price, they are no longer more attractive than a deposit account and the bond price will stop moving.

To get a 2% yield on a bond that pays out interest at $5 (which doesn't change as it is fixed for the bond), we can calculate the price by rearranging the yield equation:

Price = interest / yield × 100

Price = $5 / 2 × 100 = $250

# MACROECONOMIC AND INSTITUTIONAL CONTEXT I: THE DOMESTIC ECONOMY

**82 Included, not included, not included, included**

Aggregate demand is made up of consumption, investment, government expenditure and net exports.

**83 A**

A leftward shift would reduce output. As demand is unchanged, the same demand for a product that is produced in lower quantities would cause an increase in prices, i.e. inflation.

**84 B**

| Injections | Withdrawals |
|---|---|
| $m | $m |
| 432 | 176 |
| 249 | 503 |
| 329 | 298 |
| 1,010 | 977 |

Since injections are higher than withdrawals, the national income of the economy will start to rise.

**85 0.75**

Every time income changes by $20m, consumption changes by $15m

$$\text{Value of MPC} = \frac{\Delta C}{\Delta Y} = \frac{15}{20} = 0.75$$

Δ = change in

**86 A**

Income needs to rise by $20 million

$$\text{Value of multiplier} = \frac{1}{1-\text{MPC}} = \frac{1}{\text{MPS}} = \frac{1}{1-0.8} = \frac{1}{0.2} = 5$$

So, to achieve full employment, investment must rise by x × 5 to make $20 million x = $4 million.

**87 C**

A deflationary gap exists where planned expenditure is below the full employment level of output or income.

**88 D**

The gainers from inflation are those who have index-linked incomes and those who invest in non-financial assets.

**89 D**

A downturn in the level of economic activity is associated with the trade cycle.

**90 C**

A reduction in demand for any individual good, service or industry is associated with structural unemployment.

**91 A**

If the government were to pursue a contractionary monetary policy, they would raise interest rates so we can eliminate alternatives B and D.

They would sell securities, which would be bought by cheques from the banking sector, thereby eliminating banking liquidity.

**92 C**

An increase in the reserve asset ratio would reduce the level of liquidity in the banking sector.

**93 B**

The burden of an indirect tax on a good will fall more heavily on a consumer when the demand for a good is inelastic. For elastic goods, the consumer would choose to switch to another product rather than pay the increased price. For inelastic goods, the consumer is less likely to switch and so is more likely to have to pay the increased price, including the tax. That is why governments taxes inelastic goods such as petrol and cigarettes.

**94 C**

An expansionary fiscal policy involves reducing taxes and increasing expenditure, i.e. reducing a withdrawal and increasing an injection.

**95 D**

Alternatives A, B and C are all valid reasons why a government should have a budget deficit. A fall in unemployment should increase government revenue and reduce government expenditure.

**96 C**

Keynesians prefer to use fiscal policy to control the economy. Amending taxes or government expenditure affects demand (demand side policies).

**97 D**

Rising consumer expenditure would increase growth in the short-term but without increase in capacity on the supply side the long-term consequence would be inflation rather than growth.

**98 B**

Governments wish to control inflation because it damages international competitiveness by making local prices higher than those of international competitors.

**99 B**

If governments were seeking to reduce unemployment, they could reduce interest rates and lower taxes to stimulate growth in the economy.

**100 C**

People who are prepared to work for below the minimum wage may be prevented from doing so if there is a minimum wage because the supply of labour is being restricted. We are talking about the economic argument here not the moral one.

**101 D**

Fiscal policy relates to the government's taxation and spending plans. The creation of tax-exempt savings accounts will lower the government's taxation revenues.

**102 B**

Once an FRA has been used, the only exposure the company will have is to the FRA interest rate which, in this case, is 4%.

The operation of the FRA would be that the company borrows at the market rate on the date of the borrowing (5%) and that via the FRA, money is moved to or from the company to bring the overall exposure back to the FRA rate. In this case, the FRA would reimburse 1% of the 5% to bring the overall exposure back to the FRA rate of 4%.

**103 B**

The FRA guarantees that the company will be able to receive interest of 4% on its lending. When the lending is made, it only receives market interest of 3%. The FRA therefore operates to top-up the interest by 1% to bring the total receipt to 4%. The FRA bank must therefore pay the company 1%.

# MACROECONOMIC AND INSTITUTIONAL CONTEXT II: THE INTERNATIONAL ECONOMY

**104 D**

A trade surplus is where exports exceed imports. Trade surpluses accrue to firms, not the government.

**105 B**

Alternatives A, C and D are all examples of protectionism. A fixed exchange rate is a type of exchange rate.

**106 B**

A country imposes tariffs on foreign goods to protect employment at home.

**107 D**

A customs union is a free trade area within a certain group of countries who have a common tariff with the rest of the world.

**108 C**

If the elasticity of demand for British exports is –2, then a devaluation of sterling should lead to an increase in the total foreign currency expenditure on British goods. As the elasticity value is larger than 1, price changes of the exports (via changing the exchange rate) will lead to proportionally larger changes in the export quantities demanded. A fall in export prices through devaluation of sterling will therefore lead to a proportionally higher rise in export quantities, meaning that the overall export values will rise.

**109 –$1,175 million**

Visible trade is trade in tangible goods.

| | |
|---|---|
| Tangible exports | $35,432 |
| Tangible imports | $36,607 |
| | = –$1,175 |

**110 D**

A is a visible transaction

B is an invisible transaction (transfer of money by an individual)

C is an invisible transaction (investment income)

D is a capital flow

**111 B**

A balance of payments deficit is least likely to be corrected by increasing the value of sterling as this will make local goods more expensive, discouraging exports.

All the others reduce the level of imports (reducing aggregate demand reduces the need for items that aren't produced locally).

**112 D**

Tariffs allow domestic producers to raise their prices (as they have less competition from imports), which would generate cost push inflation.

**113 B**

Adopting common taxation policies is a stage beyond common markets. Taxation is determined by the governments' fiscal policies.

**114 A**

An economic union also has a common currency. A customs union does not have free movement of factors of production. A free trade area doesn't have a common external tariff or free movement of factors of production. A single market can include the features of a customs union, but doesn't have to.

**115 D**

Alternatives A, B and C are all correct. Statement D is half correct, increased competition should lead to lower prices.

**116 A and C**

More foreign tourism is an 'export' of services, i.e. money flows into the country. Higher commodity exports would mean goods leaving the country and cash flowing in. Both would help move the balance toward a surplus. Capital does not affect the current account. Tax receipts are not part of the balance of payments.

**117 C**

A and B are in the current account anyway, and D relates to the country's budget surplus rather than the balance of payments.

**118 A**

Import quotas restrict quantity therefore prices rise. The other three statements are generally true. In the case of C, trade protection may provoke retaliation by other countries and generally leads to a reduction in world trade.

**119 B**

Globalisation of production enables producers to take advantage of low-cost resources anywhere in the world, therefore reducing the need to concentrate production close to markets.

**120 B**

Higher tariffs will act as a barrier to international trade and deter globalisation.

**121 D**

As a consequence of globalisation, tastes are becoming more homogenised across geographies and the demand for foods that a population previously would not have had access to is rising.

**122 C**

All of the others are features of globalisation, but statement C cannot happen. The terms of trade measure the relationship between the prices of exports and imports. If they improve for one trading partner they must, by definition, deteriorate for the other trading partners.

**123 A**

One form of political risk is government measures to improve the competitiveness of national companies. The other statements are false.

**124 C**

A = Technological heading, B = Economic heading, D = Social heading.

**125**

| | |
|---|---|
| The age at which people are allowed to drink alcohol | **Legal** |
| Government tax on sales of alcohol | **Political** |
| The level of disposable income people have | **Economic** |
| People's religious beliefs and attitudes towards alcohol | **Social** |

# FINANCIAL CONTEXT OF BUSINESS II: INTERNATIONAL ASPECTS

**126 A**

B is not correct. A floating rate means that exchange rates are never certain. C is incorrect as transaction costs will still exist when one currency is exchanged for another regardless of whether a fixed or floating system is in operation. To keep a currency at a fixed rate limits a government's ability to adopt policies, which may put pressure on that rate, hence D is not correct.

**127 B**

The main advantage of a system of flexible or floating exchange rates is that it provides automatic correction of balance of payments.

**128 C**

Keeping the exchange rate low can make exports appear cheaper to foreign customers and enhance competitiveness. They can also help control inflation. For instance, if prices are rising in the local economy, strengthening the currency can make import prices cheaper. This also lowers demand for local goods and releases the inflationary price pressure on them.

**129 A and D**

A devaluation of the exchange rate for a country's currency will normally result in a reduction in the current account deficit and an increase in the level of domestic economic activity. As the currency is weakened, exports will appear cheaper to foreign customers and imports more expensive. Growing exports and falling imports mean the deficit reduces and as more local goods are produced, the local economic activity rises.

**130 C**

Overseas customers will find the country's goods cheaper, thus boosting exports. On the other hand, imported raw materials will become more expensive resulting in inflationary pressure.

**131 B**

A single currency does not necessarily ensure lower interest rates.

**132 A**

The major disadvantage of a single currency to an individual country is loss of monetary control.

**133 B**

A rise in American interest rates is likely to make funds flow from the UK to the United States, which would lead to a fall in the value of sterling (supply of sterling rises as it's swapped for dollars, demand for sterling weakens as people prefer to deposit in dollars).

**134 $140,000**

If sterling equals £1 to $1.50 a £100,000 car would be $150,000. A reduction in sterling to £1 = $1.40 would reduce the dollar price by $10,000 to $140,000.

**135 B**

B is the correct answer because this will affect the supply of sterling as UK residents sell sterling to obtain foreign currencies.

**136 A**

This is the risk of an exchange rate changing between the transaction date and the subsequent settlement date.

**137 A**

Translation risk.

**138 A**

High inflation will erode the competitiveness of exports, which will lead to lower export demand, less need for the home currency to pay for the exports and therefore will weaken the currency. An increase in interest rates can lead to a currency appreciation in the short term as investors switch their deposits to the home currency. (In the long run though, the rise in rates will end up having the same effect as high inflation mentioned above). A trade surplus means that demand for the home currency is high to pay for exports. Speculation can cause the exchange rate to move either way, so could be a reason for an appreciating currency.

**139 D**

All of these statements are true of futures contracts, when compared to forward contracts.

**140 Eady plc: loss Canadian supplier: no effect**

The Canadian supplier is unaffected as it invoices in its local currency, the Canadian dollar. It will receive the same number of Canadian $ regardless of any movements of the C$ against the £. Eady plc will have to pay more £ to purchase the C$ payable, so will suffer a loss on the weakening of sterling.

**141 C**

Leading with the payment eliminates the foreign currency exposure by removing the future liability.

Borrowing short-term in euros to meet the payment obligation in three months' time also provides cover against the exposure by converting currency at today's exchange rate, rather than at an uncertain future rate.

A forward exchange contract is a popular method of hedging against exposure.

# FINANCIAL CONTEXT OF BUSINESS III: DISCOUNTING AND INVESTMENT APPRAISAL

**142 1.9%**

Monthly rate = $(1 + \text{annual rate})^{1/12} - 1$

(The power value represents how many annual periods there are in a monthly period)

$1.253^{1/12} - 1 = 0.019$ or 1.9%

**143 C**

$(1 + 0.1/4)^4 - 1 \times 100 = 10.38\%$

$(1 + 0.12/12)^{12} - 1 \times 100 = 12.68\%$

$(1 + 0.012)^{12} - 1 \times 100 = 15.39\%$

$(1 + 0.03)^4 - 1 \times 100 = 12.55\%$

**144 D**

PV = future value × $(1 + r)^{-n}$

$r = 0.1$, $n = 4$

$10,000 × $1.1^{-4}$ = $6,830

**145 669**

| Timing | 0 | 1 | 2 | 3 |
|---|---|---|---|---|
| Cash flow ($000) | (200) | 750 | 500 | (300) |
| Discount factor | 1 | 0.909 | 0.826 | 0.751 |
| Present value | (200) | 681.75 | 413.00 | (225.3) |
| NPV (nearest $000) | 669 | | | |

**146 D**

D is the correct answer. The cash inflows are an advanced annuity as they start immediately. Use the annuity factor for 9 years and add 1 to it.

PV = 2,000 × (6.247 + 1) = $14,494 (nearest $)

**147 B**

Assuming the rate of interest stated in nominal, 6 per cent per annum in this case means ½ per cent per month, monthly ratio = 1 + (0.5/100) = 1.005

Value after 6 months = 1,000 × $1.005^6$ = 1,030.38

Therefore interest = $30.38

**148 15.96%**

The IRR is the rate at which NPV is zero. NPV drops by $928 + $628 = $1,556 as the percentage rises from 10 per cent that is by 10 per cent points. The drop per point is therefore 1,556/10 = $155.6. Since it starts at $928, the NPV will reach zero after an increase in the rate of 928/155.6 = 5.96% points. This occurs when the rate is 10% + 5.96% = 15.96%.

**149 C**

If the investment amount is equal to the PV of the perpetuity, then it will generate the correct amount. As the income is due to start in 1 year's time, we can simply multiply the $8,000 by the perpetuity factor to get the PV.

$8,000 × (1/0.05) = $160,000

**150 C**

To calculate the PV of a delayed annuity, apply the usual annuity factor (here, 6% for 10 years gives a factor of 7.360), which will discount it back to a figure as at 1 time period before the annuity starts (here, to time period 4). Then use a discount factor to discount that result back to time period 0 (here, 6% for 4 years leads to a discount factor of 0.792)

$5,000 × 7.360 × 0.792 = $29,146.

You may prefer to do the calculation by taking the annuity factor for years 1 to 14 and deducting the annuity factor for years 1 to 4 before multiplying by the $5,000 – this will give the same answer (taking roundings into account):

$5,000 × (9.295 – 3.465) = $29,150

**151 B**

Equate PVs: sum now = PV of future annuity

Let x = annual repayment

Present value of 8 repayments of x at 9% = $50,000

From tables 5.535 × x = $50,000

$$x = \frac{£50{,}000}{5.535} = \$9{,}033$$

**152 D**

| Year | Cash ($000) | 17% discount factor | Present value ($000) |
|---|---|---|---|
| 0 | (400) | 1.000 | (400.00) |
| 1 | 210 | 0.855 | 179.55 |
| 2 | 240 | 0.731 | 175.44 |
| 3 | 320 | 0.624 | 199.68 |
| | | | 154.67 |

**153 14%**

$$10 + \frac{\$17{,}706}{(17{,}706 - -£4{,}317)} \times (15 - 10) = 14\%$$

**154 20%**

At 25%

| Year | Cash | 25% | PV |
|---|---|---|---|
| | $ | | $ |
| 0 | (75,000) | | (75,000) |
| 1 – 5 | 25,000 | 2.689 | 67,225 |
| | | | (7,775) |

$$IRR = 15 + \frac{8{,}800}{(8{,}800 - -7{,}775)} \times (25 - 15)$$

$$IRR = 15 + \frac{8{,}800}{16{,}575} \times 10$$

IRR = 20.31% therefore 20% to the nearest 1%

**155 C**

As first payment is due now, it is an advanced annuity. Use the annuity factor for 9 years at 8% (6.247) and add 1 to the annuity factor to get the present value.

NPV = $1,000 × (1 + 6.247) = $7,247

**156 B**

B is the correct answer because NPV shows the potential increase in shareholder wealth, in cash terms. Shareholders prefer cash over profits, as this directly increases their wealth.

**157 D**

The PV of the annuity must be equal to the amount invested. The PV is calculated by multiplying the annual cash value by the 10-year, 7% annuity factor of 7.024.

Thus, annual cash value × 7.024 = $65,000

Annual cash value = $65,000/7.024 = $9,254 or $9,250 to the nearest $10

**158 C**

If the net present value is positive at 15 per cent and negative at 20 per cent, it must be zero somewhere between the two.

**159 A**

| Year | Cash | 11% | PV |
|---|---|---|---|
| | $ | | $ |
| 0 | (300,000) | | (300,000) |
| 1 – 10 | 40,000 | 5.889 | 235,560 |
| | | | (64,440) |

**160 A and B**

A True because the NPV profile of project Y crosses the discount rate axis beyond that for project X.

B True – at discount rates less than 15% project X has a higher NPV and is therefore preferred.

C and D False – at discount rates less than 15% project X is preferred, whereas at rates greater than 15% project Y is preferred.

**161 B**

| Project | A | B | C |
|---|---|---|---|
| NPV @ 10% | $2,680 | $925 | $(220) |

Therefore, undertake A and B

# INFORMATIONAL CONTEXT OF BUSINESS I: SUMMARISING AND ANALYSING DATA

**162 D**

The other graphs/charts rely on some correlation between the variables. A scatter graph is more likely to illustrate a random pattern or non-relationship.

**163 D**

A simple bar chart would show five bars illustrating the different salaries in different regions.

**164 C**

The sales revenue is dependent on the money spent on advertising. The more advertising that is done the higher the sales revenue should be. Not vice versa. Dependent values are plotted on the y axis and independent ones on the x axis.

**165 D**

A bar chart is a good way of illustrating total sales month by month. The length of the bar each month is a measure of total sales. The bar can be divided into three parts, to show the amount of sales achieved for each of the three products. This is called a component bar chart.

**166 C**

Cumulative frequencies are plotted against the upper class boundaries.

**167 D**

Note that the compound bar chart in the question is not the best type of chart from which to read this information. A multiple bar chart, with separate bars for each month, would have made it easier to determine the correct answer. Compound bar charts are useful when the total is important, such as the total for each salesperson over the three-month period.

**168 B**

The histogram must show the relationship of the rectangles to the frequencies by reference to the area.

**169**

| | **True** | **False** |
|---|---|---|
| Area 3 shows the best performance in Q3 | ✓ | |
| Area 2 sales are consistent quarter on quarter | | ✓ |
| Q4 has the largest volume of sales across all areas | ✓ | |
| Area 1 shows the best performance in Q2 | ✓ | |

**170 A**

All statements are true except A. Histograms plot frequency against class size. The area of the bar plotted for each class size represents the frequency for that class size.

**171 14**

Height = 8 for frequency of 16, so for frequency of 28, height should be 28/16*8 = 14.

**172 D**

Information needs to be timely – i.e. available in time for when it is needed. This is not necessarily the same as having the information available quickly, although with on-line Internet connections, it is increasingly common for information to be needed quickly.

**173 A**

Qualitative data is normally non-numerical. Information comes from both internal and external sources. Operational information is usually short-term (current) in nature. Quantitative data will be as accurate as possible.

**174 A**

All of the others have been processed in some way and are information.

**175 True, False, True**

The information should be sufficiently accurate given time and cost constraints. Managers should be made aware of the degree of accuracy of the information.

**176 D**

Useful management information does not necessarily have to be presented in report format, supported by calculations or communicated in writing.

**177 D**

Data consists of numbers, letters, symbols, raw facts, events and transactions that have been recorded but not yet processed into a form that is suitable for making decisions. Information is data that has been processed in such a way that it has a meaning to the person who receives it, who may then use it to improve the quality of decision-making.

**178 B and D**

Option A is incorrect in that Big Data does not refer to any specific financial amount. Option C is also incorrect. Big Data can indeed come from many sources, but this is too narrow a definition. Big Data refers to the large volume of data, the many sources of data and the many types of data.

**179 B, C and D**

Note that the increasing use of electronic devices makes Big Data collection easier. Many organisations successfully gather information from social media sites such as Facebook and Twitter and use it to great effect within their decision-making processes.

# MACROECONOMIC AND INSTITUTIONAL CONTEXT III: INDEX NUMBERS

**180 B**

If an index of average gross earnings with a base year 2011 and at constant 2011 prices (meaning the prices have not changed between 2011 and 2016) is calculated to be 107 by 2016, it means that 7 per cent more goods and services can be bought by average earnings over a 5-year period.

**181 C**

The correct answers are (ii) and (iv). If you subtract 100 from an index number, it gives the percentage increase since the base year. Equally, if you divide an index number by 100, it gives the ratio of current values to base-year values.

**182 A**

| Quarter | 'Real' sales |
|---|---|
| 1 | (109/100) × 100 = 109.0 |
| 2 | (120/110) × 100 = 109.1 |
| 3 | (132/121) × 100 = 109.1 |
| 4 | (145/133) × 100 = 109.0 |

The 'real' series is approximately constant and keeping up with inflation.

**183 133**

Multiply the individual indices by their weightings, add the results together and then divide by the total weighting.

All items index = [(50 × 140) + (30 × 130) + (20 × 120)]/100 = 133

**184 A**

Multiply the individual indices by their weightings, add the results together and then divide by the total weighting.

Let the index for food = f

$$\text{weighted index} = \frac{\sum(\text{weight} \times \text{index})}{\sum\text{weight}}$$

$$127 = \frac{[(130 \times 7) + (f \times 3)]}{10}$$

127 × 10 = (130 × 7) + (f × 3)

1270 = 910 + 3f

3f = 1270 – 910

3f = 360

f = 120

**182 $563.22**

In the base year, the price = $490/87 × 100 = $563.22

**186 B and C**

An index of 102 means that prices have risen by 2 per cent, which in turn means that current values are 1.02 times their values in the base year, on average.

**187 A**

$2,000 × 120/160 = $1,500

**188 D**

$$\text{Relative price index} = \frac{\sum [w\times (P_1/P_0)]}{\sum w}\times 100$$

The question asks for base weighting using quantities, so last year's quantities are used as the weighting

| Product | $P_1/P_0$ | Weighting (w) | $w \times P_1/P_0$ |
|---|---|---|---|
| Bread | 1.25 | 800 | 1,000 |
| Milk | 1.5 | 4,000 | 6,000 |
| Biscuits | 1.1 | 750 | 825 |
| Total | | 5,550 | 7,825 |

Index = 7,825/5,550 × 100 = 141.0

**189 151.8**

$$\text{Relative quantity index} = \frac{\sum [w\times (Q_1/Q_0)]}{\sum w}\times 100$$

The question asks for base weighting using prices, so last year's prices are used as the weighting

| Product | $Q_1/Q_0$ | Weighting (w) | $w \times P_1/P_0$ |
|---|---|---|---|
| Bread | 1.25 | 1.20 | 1.5 |
| Milk | 1.25 | 0.60 | 0.75 |
| Biscuits | 2.0 | 1.00 | 2.0 |
| Total | | 2.80 | 4.25 |

Index = 4.25/2.80 × 100 = 151.8

**190 B**

$$\text{Relative price index} = \frac{\sum [w\times (P_1/P_0)]}{\sum w}\times 100$$

The question asks for current weighting using quantities, so this year's quantities are used as the weighting

| Product | $P_1/P_0$ | Weighting (w) | $w \times P_1/P_0$ |
|---|---|---|---|
| Bread | 1.25 | 1,000 | 1,250 |
| Milk | 1.5 | 5,000 | 7,500 |
| Biscuits | 1.1 | 1,500 | 1,650 |
| Total | | 7,500 | 10,400 |

Index = 10,400/7,500 × 100 = 138.7

**191 148.6**

Relative quantity index = $\frac{\sum [w\times (Q_1/Q_0)]}{\sum w} \times 100$

The question asks for current weighting using prices, so this year's prices are used as the weighting

| Product | $Q_1/Q_0$ | Weighting (w) | w × $P_1/P_0$ |
|---|---|---|---|
| Bread | 1.25 | 1.50 | 1.875 |
| Milk | 1.25 | 0.90 | 1.125 |
| Biscuits | 2.0 | 1.10 | 2.20 |
| Total | | 3.50 | 5.20 |

Index = 5.20/3.50 × 100 = 148.6

# INFORMATIONAL CONTEXT OF BUSINESS II: INTER-RELATIONSHIPS BETWEEN VARIABLES

**192 B**

Equation of line is y = a + bx

$$b \; \frac{(n\sum xy - \sum x \sum y)}{(n\sum x^2 - (\sum x)^2)}$$

$$b \; \frac{(12 \times 14{,}200) - (560 \times 85)}{12 \times 62{,}500 - 560 \times 560} = \frac{122{,}800}{436{,}400}$$

b = 0.281

$$a = \bar{y} - b\bar{x} \text{ or } \frac{\sum y}{n} - b\frac{\sum x}{n}$$

$$a \; \frac{85}{12} - 0.281 \times \frac{560}{12} = -6.03$$

Regression line is y = –6.03 + 0.281x

**193 A**

$a = \bar{y} - b\bar{x}$

$$a = \frac{\sum y}{n} - \frac{b\sum x}{n} = \frac{183{,}000}{5} - \frac{4{,}200 \times 21}{5} = [36{,}600 - 17{,}640] = 18{,}960$$

If there are 2 salesmen in the month, expected costs will be: 18,960 + (4,200 × 2) = 27,360

**194 B**

Σx = Σ Advertising expenditure = 100,000 (independent variable)

Σy = Σ Sales revenue = 600,000 (dependent variable)

n = number of pairs of data = 5

**195 A, D and F**

Y = 5.0913 + 0.2119X

When X increases by 1, Y increases by 0.2119 and since Y is measured in $000 this means that variable cost is (0.2119 × $1,000) $211.90 per unit. When X = 0, Y = 5.0913 which means that fixed costs are $5,091.3

**196 $5,800,000**

When $150,000 is spent on advertising, X = 150 and Y = 4,000 + 12 × 150 = 5,800.

Forecast sales = 5,800 ($000)

**197 A and B**

Statement C is incorrect: x = 0 is outside the range of the data.

Statement D is incorrect: when x increases by $1, y increases by $4.30 from the regression equation.

Statement E is incorrect: you need to square the correlation coefficient to get the coefficient of determination to make such statements.

**198 B**

For a perfect positive correlation, we want the value of r to be equal to 1.

**199 A**

Coefficient of determination = $r^2$ = 0.6 × 0.6 = 0.36 = 36%

**200 B**

The coefficient of determination ($r^2$) explains the percentage variation in the dependent variable that is explained by the independent variable.

**201 D**

| Product | Customer X | Customer Y | d | $d^2$ |
|---|---|---|---|---|
| A | 4 | 2 | 2 | 4 |
| B | 5 | 3 | 2 | 4 |
| C | 2 | 1 | 1 | 1 |
| D | 1 | 4 | –3 | 9 |
| E | 3 | 5 | –2 | 4 |
| F | 6 | 6 | 0 | 0 |
| | | | 0 | 22 |

$$R \text{ (rank correlation)} = 1 - \frac{6\sum d^2}{n(n^2 - 1)} = 1 - \frac{(6 \times 22)}{(6 \times 35)} = 1 - \frac{132}{210} = 1 - 0.63$$

= 0.37

**202 –0.85**

$$R \text{ (rank correlation)} = 1 - \frac{6\sum d^2}{n(n^2-1)} = 1 - \frac{(6 \times 304.5)}{(10 \times 99)} = 1 - 1.8455 = -0.85 \text{ (to 2dp)}$$

**203 A and D**

The rank correlation is positive and hence values of Y typically increase as values of X increase. Numerically its value is close to 1 and hence the link between X and Y values is very strong. We can never deduce cause and effect from any correlation coefficient, however large, so (F) is incorrect as are the numerical comments in (B) and (C). (E) is incorrect because a linear relationship between ranks of values does not necessarily imply one between the values themselves.

# INFORMATIONAL CONTEXT OF BUSINESS III: FORECASTING

**204 D**

| | | |
|---|---|---|
| Actual value | = | Trend × seasonal factor |
| Seasonally adjusted figure | = | Estimate of the trend |
| | = | Actual value/seasonal factor |
| | = | 2,200/0.97 = 2,268 |

It seems likely that the stated trend of 2,000 is incorrect.

**205 C**

Seasonally-adjusted data = actual results/seasonal factor

= $25,000/0.78 = $32,051

**206 D**

Rebased price (152/127) × 100 = 119.69

**207 C**

y = 7.112 + 3.949x

Seasonal variation = 1.12 × trend

For month 19

y = 7.112 + (3.949 × 19) × 1.12

y = 92

**208 80**

Predicted value (using an additive model) = predicted trend + cyclical component.

2019 will be year 1 of the cycle (2016 = 2, 2017 = 3, 2018 = 4). Therefore, predicted value = 70 + 10 = 80.

**209 D**

| Quarter | Value of x | | Trend units | | | Forecast sales units |
|---|---|---|---|---|---|---|
| 1 | 25 | y = (26 × 25) + 8,850 | 9,500 | × 85% | = | 8,075.0 |
| 4 | 28 | y = (26 × 28) + 8,850 | 9,578 | × 115% | = | 11,014.7 |

Difference between Q1 and Q4 budgeted sales = 11,014.7 – 8,075.0 = 2,939.7 units

**210 The overhead cost for RP for month 240 is $39,000**

Number of orders = [100,000 + (30 × 240)] × 1.08 = 115,776

Overhead cost = $10,000 + ($0.25 × 115,776) = $38,944

Answer is $39,000

**211 D**

| | | |
|---|---|---|
| Trend | = | 9.72 + (5.816 × 23) |
| | = | 143.488 |
| Seasonal factor | + | 6.5 |
| Forecast | | 149.988 |

To the nearest whole unit, the forecast number of units to be sold is 150.

**212 300,750 units**

We have been given the trend equation. We need to plug in the value for x so that we can find y.

X is the time period reference number and for the first quarter of year 1 is 1. The time period reference number for the third quarter of year 7 is 27. (Just keep adding 1 to the time period reference number for each new quarter, thus quarter 2, year 1, x = 2; quarter 3, year 1, x = 3; quarter 4, year 1, x = 4; quarter 1, year 2, x = 5, etc.)

y = 25,000 + 6,500 × 27 = 200,500 units

This is the trend we now need to multiply by the seasonal variation for quarter 3:

Forecast = 200,500 × 150/100 = 300,750 units.

Section 3

# PRACTICE ASSESSMENT QUESTIONS

1 The following financial data refers to a company.

| | | |
|---|---|---|
| Capital employed | 1.1.X6 | $900,000 |
| Capital employed | 31.12.X6 | $1,100,000 |
| Gross profits for year ending | 31.12.X6 | $105,000 |
| Interest payments year ending | 31.12.X6 | $20,000 |
| Tax paid on profits year ending | 31.12.X6 | $15,000 |

**What is the value of the rate of return on capital for this company? Give your answer as a decimal, to one decimal place.**

[ ] %

2 **All of the following are essential features of a market economy EXCEPT which ONE?**

A Private ownership of productive resources

B Allocation of resources by the price mechanism

C Absence of entry and exit barriers to and from industries

D Prices determined by market forces

3 **Consider the following data for a proposed investment project.**

| | |
|---|---|
| Capital cost of the project | $7,000 |
| Life of the investment | 3 years |
| Scrap value of the capital at end of Year 3 | $500 |
| Income generated by the project | |
| Year 1 | $2,000 |
| Year 2 | $3,000 |
| Year 3 | $2,000 |

**What is the net present value for the project assuming a discount rate of 10%? Give your answer in $s to the nearest $.**

$ [ ]

4 **All of the following would be expected to raise share values EXCEPT which one?**

A An announcement of higher than expected profits

B A reduction in corporation tax

C A rise in interest rates

D A rise in share prices on overseas stock markets

**5 The principal – agent problem refers to**

A situations where a company's selling agents are not meeting the company's main sales targets

B problems arising when a principal delegates authority to an agent but cannot ensure the agent will always act in his/her interest

C cases where companies lack knowledge on particular markets and have to seek agents to act on their behalf

D the power a large company may exert over suppliers when it is the dominant buyer of that supplier's output

**6 If a business currently sells 10,000 units of its product per month at $10 per unit and the demand for its product has a price elasticity of –2.5, calculated using the non-average arc method, a rise in the price of the product to $11 will**

A raise total revenue by $7,250

B reduce total revenue by $17,500

C reduce total revenue by $25,000

D raise total revenue by $37,500

**7 If the market supply curve for a good is inelastic, using the non-average arc method, an increase in demand will**

A raise total sales proportionately more than it will raise the market price

B raise total sales proportionately less than it will raise the market price

C raise the market price but leave total sales unaffected

D raise total sales but leave the market price unchanged

**8 Which TWO of the following would be most likely to be classified as BOTH private sector AND profit seeking?**

A A charity that raises funds from the public for medical research

B A limited company that sells motor parts

C A co-operative supermarket

D A school operated by a local government authority

E A partnership that offers accountancy services

**9 A good which is characterised by both rivalry and excludability is called**

A a public good

B a private good

C a government good

D an external good

**10 Which ONE of the following is the best example of a merit good?**

A Street lighting

B A national defence force

C Company cars for top sales executives

D A system of public libraries

**11 Which TWO of the following statements about the privatisation of state industries are true?**

A Privatisation increases the commercial pressure on the business to make a profit

B Privatisation ensures the business faces competition and so encourages greater efficiency

C Privatisation is a means of solving the principal – agent problem

D Privatisation is likely to make the business more responsive to needs of its customers

**12 All of the following are examples of where externalities are likely to occur EXCEPT which ONE?**

A A business providing training schemes for its employees

B Government expenditure on vaccination programmes for infectious diseases

C Attending a concert given by a government funded orchestra

D Private motorists driving cars in city centres

**13 Whenever government intervention prevents prices from reaching their equilibrium level, the result will always include ALL of the following EXCEPT which ONE?**

A Shortages or surpluses

B Demand and supply not equal

C Reduced profits for producers

D Resources not allocated by price

**14 A fall in the price of a good accompanied by a rise in the quantity sold would result from**

A a decrease in supply

B an increase in demand

C a decrease in demand

D an increase in supply

**15 Which one of the following is NOT a characteristic of not-for-profit organisations?**

A They need efficient and effective management

B They make financial surpluses and deficits

C They have a range of stakeholders

D The absence of any principal – agent problem

**16 It is not always a legal requirement for a company to have a strong system of corporate governance.**

**True or false?**

**17 A business could use all of the following to finance a lack of synchronisation in its short-term payments and receipts EXCEPT which ONE?**

A A bank overdraft

B Trade credit

C Its cash reserves

D A hire purchase agreement

**18 Which TWO of the following financial instruments appearing on a commercial bank's balance sheet would be an asset for the bank?**

A Advances

B Money held in reserve at the central bank

C Deposit accounts

D Shareholder capital

**19 If banks are required to keep a reserve assets ratio of 10% and also wish to keep a margin of liquid reserves of 10%, by how much would deposits ultimately rise by if they acquire an additional $10,000 of reserve assets?**

A $100,000

B $50,000

C $10,000

D $5,000

**20 If a commercial bank reallocates some of its assets from less profitable to more profitable ones,**

A the bank's liquidity will be increased

B the safety of the bank's assets will be increased

C the bank's liquidity will be decreased

D the liquidity and safety of the bank's assets will be unaffected

**21 Which of the following statements about the relationship between bond prices and bond yields is true?**

A They vary positively

B They vary inversely

C They vary inversely or positively depending on business conditions

D They are not related

**22 Under a regime of flexible exchange rates, which one of the following would lead to a rise in the exchange rate for a country's currency?**

A A shift in the country's balance of payments current account towards a surplus

B A rise in interest rates in other countries

C An increasing balance of trade deficit

D The central bank buying foreign exchange on the foreign exchange market

**23 Exchange rates are determined by supply and demand for currencies in the foreign exchange market. Which TWO of the following would be part of the supply of a country's currency?**

A Payments for imports into the country

B Inflows of capital into the country

C Purchases of foreign currency by the country's central bank

D Foreign tourists visiting the country

**24** Each of the following is a source of funds for capital investment for business except one.

**Which ONE is the EXCEPTION?**

A Commercial banks

B Internally generated funds

C The stock market

D The central bank

**25 The linking of net savers with net borrowers is known as**

A the savings function

B financial intermediation

C financial regulation

D a store of value

**26 If a consumer price index rises, it shows that**

A the value of the currency has increased

B real consumer income has fallen

C all prices in the economy have risen

D the purchasing power of money has decreased

**27 The main function of the money market is to**

A enable businesses and governments to obtain liquidity

B encourage saving

C permit the efficient buying and selling of shares

D deal in credit instruments of more than one year maturity

**28 The effects of low real interest rates include all of the following EXCEPT which ONE?**

A Credit based sales will tend to be high

B Nominal costs of borrowing will always be low

C Business activity will tend to increase

D Investment will be encouraged

**29 Which ONE of the following would cause the value of the multiplier to fall?**

A A fall in the level of government expenditure

B A rise in the marginal propensity to consume

C A fall in business investment

D A rise in the marginal propensity to save

**30 The recession phase of the trade cycle will normally be accompanied by all of the following EXCEPT which ONE?**

A A rise in the rate of inflation

B A fall in the level of national output

C An improvement in the trade balance

D A rise in the level of unemployment

**31 Match the types of unemployment in the drop-down list below to the following definitions.**

| Definition of unemployment | Type of unemployment |
|---|---|
| (i) Unemployment that occurs in particular industries and arises from long-term changes in the patterns of demand and supply | |
| (ii) Unemployment associated with industries or regions where the demand for labour and wage rates regularly rise and fall over the year | |

Drop down list:

| |
|---|
| **Structural unemployment** |
| **Cyclical unemployment** |
| **Real wage (classical) unemployment** |
| **Frictional unemployment** |
| **Seasonal unemployment** |

**32 All of the following will lead to a fall in the level of economic activity in an economy EXCEPT which ONE?**

A A rise in cyclical unemployment

B A fall in business investment

C A decrease in government expenditure

D A rise in interest rates

**33 Supply side policy is designed to**

A raise the level of aggregate monetary demand in the economy

B manage the money supply in the economy

C improve the ability of the economy to produce goods and services

D reduce unemployment by limiting the supply of labour

**34 Indicate whether each of the following taxes are direct taxes or indirect taxes.**

| **Type of tax** | **Direct** | **Indirect** |
|---|---|---|
| Income tax | | |
| Value added tax | | |
| Corporation tax | | |
| National insurance (social security tax) | | |

**35 The following diagram shows the aggregate demand curve (AD) and the aggregate supply curve (AS) for an economy:**

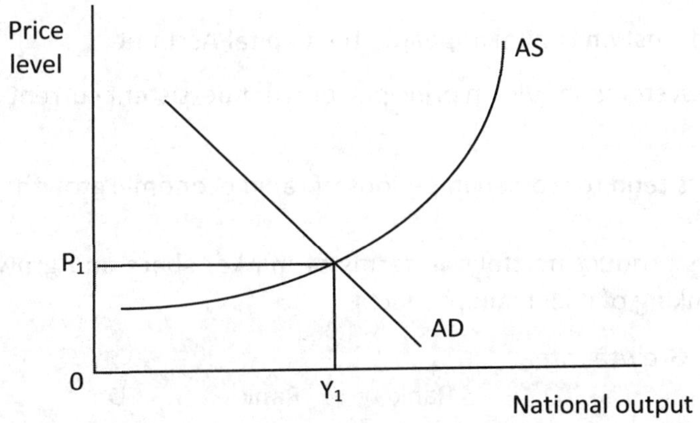


With reference to the diagram:

A __________ supply shock would shift the __________ curve to the left and cause the rate of inflation to increase. However, the level of __________ would fall. A(n) __________ fiscal policy would shift the __________ curve to the right leading to a __________ in both the level of national output and the rate of inflation.

**Drag and drop the following words and phrases to fill in the gaps in the above passage.**

| | |
|---|---|
| **Positive** | **Negative** |
| **Expansionary** | **Deflationary** |
| **Aggregate Demand** | **Aggregate Supply** |
| **Rise** | **Fall** |
| **Inflation** | **National Output** |

**36 All of the following will encourage the process of the globalisation of production EXCEPT which ONE?**

A Reductions in international transport costs

B Higher levels of tariffs

C Reduced barriers to international capital movements

D Increased similarity in demand patterns between countries

**37 Which ONE of the following does not drive globalisation?**

A The collapse of single markets

B The growth of global firms

C Cheaper labour in a foreign country

D Improved information and communications technology

**38 Which TWO of the following statements about the balance of payments are true?**

A A deficit on a country's balance of payments current account can be financed by a surplus of invisible trade

B Flows of profits and interest on capital appear in the Capital Account

C Flexible exchange rate systems should, in principle, prevent persistent current account imbalances

D Current account deficits tend to worsen in periods of rapid economic growth

39 F plc is looking to analyse its product portfolio in terms of market share and growth. The following table shows the ranking of its 5 main products.

| Product | Market share (%) | Growth rate (%) | Rank | Rank | D |
|---|---|---|---|---|---|
| | *y* | *x* | *y* | *x* | |
| V | 30 | 5.1 | 2.5 | 2 | 0.5 |
| W | 36 | 3.8 | 1 | 3 | –2 |
| X | 21 | 6.2 | 5 | 1 | 4 |
| Y | 30 | 1.4 | 2.5 | 5 | –2.5 |
| Z | 27 | 2.3 | 4 | 4 | 0 |

**What is the coefficient of rank correlation?**

A 1

B –0.66

C –0.33

D –1

**40 All of the following are benefits which all countries gain when adopting a single currency such as the Euro, EXCEPT which ONE?**

A Reduced transactions costs

B Increased price transparency

C Lower interest rates

D Reduced exchange rate uncertainty

**41 Which TWO of the following events would raise inflation?**

**Assume that the economy is close to full employment.**

A A rise (appreciation) in the exchange for the country's currency

B A significant increase in the money supply

C The removal of house prices from the consumer price index

D A rise in business expectations leading to an increase in investment

**42 Compared to a fixed exchange rate system, an economy will benefit from a flexible exchange rate system because**

A it enables businesses to vary their export prices

B governments will not have to deflate the economy when balance of payments deficits occur

C it reduces the cost of acquiring foreign exchange

D it ensures that businesses never become uncompetitive in international markets

**43 All of the following statements are true EXCEPT which ONE?**

A Import quotas tend to reduce prices

B Trade protection tends to reduce consumer choice

C Trade protection tends to reduce exports

D Tariffs tend to reduce competition

**44 Who are the gainers from inflation?**

(i) Borrowers

(ii) Savers

(iii) Those who hold cash

(iv) Those who invest in assets

A (i), (ii)

B (i), (iii)

C (ii), (iii)

D (i), (iv)

**Questions 45 and 46 are based on the following scenario:**

| | |
|---|---|
| Company X plc | |
| Share price beginning of the year | \$1.20 |
| Share price end of the year | \$1.50 |
| Dividend paid | 12 cents per share |
| Net profit before and after taxation | \$25,000 and \$20,000 |
| No. of ordinary shares | 100,000 |
| Interest paid | \$10,000 |

**45 The dividend yield was:**

A 7.5%

B 10%

C 12%

D 14%

**46 The earnings per share was:**

A 5c

B 10c

C 15c

D 20c

**47 Which one of the following will shift the supply curve for Good X to the right?**

A A government subsidy in the production of Good X

B A decrease in labour productivity in the production of Good X

C An increase in the price of materials used to produce Good X

D An increase in real wages paid to producers of Good X

**48 Which of the following would be regarded as long-term capital?**

(i) Ordinary shares

(ii) Debentures

(iii) Convertible bond

A (i) only

B (i), (ii)

C (ii), (iii)

D (i), (ii), (iii)

**49 Which of the following are examples of protectionism?**

(i) Import quota

(ii) Import tariff

(iii) Export subsidy

A (i) only

B (i), (ii)

C (ii), (iii)

D (i), (ii) and (iii)

**50 Which of the following would cause a withdrawal from the circular flow of funds?**

(i) Increase in imports

(ii) Increase in taxes

(iii) Reduction in government expenditure

A (i)

B (i), (ii)

C (i), (iii)

D (i), (ii) and (iii)

**51 If the central bank was to increase interest rates, what would be the least likely economic consequence?**

A The exchange rate would rise

B The price of non-financial assets would fall

C Inflation should fall

D Consumer expenditure would rise

**52 In the circular flow model of the economy, a state of equilibrium is reached when**

A levels of imports and exports are equal

B levels of injections and withdrawals are equal

C levels of government spending and taxation are equal

D levels of consumption and income are equal

**53 Which ONE of the following is an example of an external economy of scale for a business enterprise?**

A A locally available trained labour force

B Technical economies of scale

C Bulk buying

D Financial economies of scale

**54 P is considering outsourcing several non-core functions within her business. Which TWO of the following statements regarding this decision are incorrect?**

A It will reduce transaction costs within P's business

B It may reduce the cost of these functions to P

C P may benefit from the skills and expertise of the suppliers she chooses

D P will be able to focus her time on the core activities within her business

E P can easily bring the functions back in house at a later date if the outsourcing proves ineffective

F It may help P to deal with areas within the business she currently lacks the skills to run effectively

**55 The three types of product sold by a shop have price indices of 105, 103 and 102 compared with last year. Find the weighted average index for the products, to one decimal place, using quantities as weights if the quantities sold are in the ratio 3:2:1.**

| |
|---|
| |

**56** In a time series analysis, the trend Y is given by the regression equation Y = 462 + 0.34t where t denotes the quarters of years with 1st quarter of 2013 as t = 1.

The average seasonal variations are as follow

| Quarter | Q1 | Q2 | Q3 | Q4 |
|---|---|---|---|---|
| Variation | 20% | 0 | –20% | +40% |

**Use the multiplicative model to predict the actual value for a 1st quarter of 2017 (give your answer to the nearest whole number)**

| |
|---|
| |

**57 A graphical presentation of classified data in which the number of items in each class is represented by the area of the bar is called**

A an ogive

B a histogram

C a bar chart

D a compound bar chart

**58** Rutherford Co, whose home currency is the New Zealand Dollar (NZD), trades regularly with customers and suppliers in a number of different countries and currencies. As well as other transactions, the company expects to receive NZD 200,000 in three months' time from an Australian customer and to have to pay EUR 500,000 to a French supplier in six months' time.

**What type of foreign exchange risk exposure is Rutherford Co exposed to due to the receipt from the Australian customer?**

A Transaction risk

B Economic risk

C Translation risk

D Rutherford does not face any foreign exchange risk due to the receipt

**59 Which TWO of the following statements are correct?**

A Economic risk, in the exchange rate risk context, is related to the problems of government changing the macroeconomic environment (inflation, GDP growth etc.).

B Foreign exchange transaction risk in overseas trading relates to the problems of counterparties failing to fulfil obligations.

C The forward foreign exchange market is one in which a deal is arranged to exchange currencies at some future date at a price agreed now.

D The spot market is one in which transactions take place and delivery (fulfilment of the agreement) always occurs within minutes.

E Translation risk occurs when the reported performance of an overseas subsidiary is distorted in the consolidated financial statements due to a change in exchange rates.

**60 What is the NPV of buying an asset that will generate income of $1,200 at the end of each year for eight years? The price of the asset is $6,200 and the annual interest rate is 10%.**

A –$202

B $202

C $3,400

D –$1,721.53

Section 4

# ANSWERS TO PRACTICE ASSESSMENT QUESTIONS

**1 10.5%**

ROCE = profits before interest and tax/average capital employed × 100

Average capital employed = ($900k + $1,100k)/2 = $1,000k

ROCE = $105k/$1,000k × 100% = 10.5%

**2 C**

Market economies may have barriers to entry/exit

**3 –824 OR -826 OR -827**

NPV = –$7,000 + ($2,000 × $1.1^{-1}$) + ($3,000 × $1.1^{-2}$) + ($2,500 × $1.1^{-3}$) = –$824

Alternatively, using the discount factors from the tables:

NPV = –$7,000 + ($2,000 × 0.909) + ($3,000 × 0.826) + ($2,500 × 0.751) = -$826.50 (rounding to either -$826 or -$827 would be appropriate).

**4 C**

An increase in interest rates will reduce profits, net cash inflows and, hence, share values.

**5 B**

By definition

**6 B**

- Elastic demand ⇒ % decrease in Q > % increase in price ⇒ increase in price will result in a fall in revenue
- Existing revenue = 10,000 × $10 = $100,000
- % change in price = +10%, so % change in demand = –2.5 × 10 = –25%
- New demand = 75% × 10,000 = 7,500
- New revenue = 7,500 × $11 = $82,500, a fall of $17,500

**7 B**

Inelastic $\Rightarrow$ % increase in Q < % increase in price due to the increase in demand.

With inelastic supply, the supply curve is relatively steep. If demand increases (the demand curve shifts to the right), the equilibrium price will move sharply up the steep supply curve, but the equilibrium quantity supplied will show a smaller movement. This means that while the price rises sharply, the total quantity supplied (and sold) will move by a smaller proportion.

**8 B and E**

Private sector suggests an organisation that is not controlled by government. This means that D cannot be correct.

Charities and co-operatives are not set up to seek profits, which leaves us with the limited company and the partnership. Both are business structures that will likely be in the private sector AND will be seeking profits.

**9 B**

By definition

**10 D**

Merit goods tend to have positive externalities and should generally be available to all.

**11 A and D**

Private businesses can be a monopoly with no competition. Privatisation is a cause of the principal – agent problem, for instance with private companies whose shares are traded on the stock market. These can have thousands of shareholders (principals) but run by a select few (agents).

**12 C**

Externalities are social costs or benefits that are not automatically included in the supply and demand curves for a product or service. Social benefits arise when there is a wider external benefit, such as when employees are trained by a business and take that extra knowledge to subsequent employment, or where government vaccination schemes reduce the level of disease, which benefits those who are not vaccinated. Social costs are where the cost is felt by those not providing or consuming the product or service, such as those who suffer from pollution due to others driving cars in city centres.

**13 C**

At equilibrium, supply and demand are equal, so if equilibrium is not reached they will not be equal and there will either be a shortage or surplus of one or the other. Only at equilibrium are resources automatically allocated by price. In a situation of minimum pricing, producers can make higher profits than if there was no price intervention.

**14 D**

To answer this question, you may wish to draw a demand and supply curve and then consider where the new equilibrium point would be (where the curves intersect) after the move described in each of the answer options.

A decrease in supply would shift the supply curve to the left and would move the equilibrium position to a point of higher price and reduced supply.

An increase in demand would move the demand curve to the right and would lead to an expansion of supply and a higher price point.

A decrease in demand would move the demand curve to the left and would lead to a contraction of supply and a lower price point.

An increase in supply shifts the supply curve to the right and leads to an equilibrium point that has increased quantities and a lower price.

**15 D**

NFP organisations can still have principal-agent issues – e.g. managers not representing trustees' wishes to maximise benefits for the recipients of a charity's activities.

**16 TRUE**

Whether or not compliance is a legal requirement depends on the size of the company (smaller or unlisted companies may be exempt) as well as the country the company operates in (the US has corporate governance as a legal requirement, while the UK sees it as a set of best practice guidelines).

**17 D**

An HP agreement is used as a method of medium-term finance.

**18 A and B**

C and D are liabilities from the bank's perspective.

**19 B**

$$\text{Credit creation multiplier} = \frac{1}{\text{reserve ratio}} = \frac{1}{0.2} = 5$$

Change in total deposits = 5 × 10,000 = 50,000

**20 C**

More profitable investments are likely to have lower liquidity.

**21 B**

Bond yield = interest/market value (price) × 100

**22 A**

A surplus on the current account would indicate that exports exceed imports so demand for the domestic currency would exceed supply, all other factors being equal.

B and C would lead to a fall in demand for the currency and B, C and D would create demand for other currencies – all leading to a weakening of the home currency.

**23 A and C**

B and D represent demand.

**24 D**

A central bank does not typically lend to businesses.

**25 B**

Such linking is performed by financial intermediaries, such as banks. Without them, those who need money (net borrowers) and those who have a surplus of money they wish to invest (net savers) would find it difficult to find each other.

**26 D**

The CPI relates to the movement in average prices of goods over time. As it has risen, the goods on average (but not necessarily all of them) have become more expensive and therefore the same amount of money will now purchase fewer goods – the purchasing power of the money has fallen.

**27 A**

Money markets are essentially short term. While savers (B) could be looking at short term saving, they will be more concerned about the longer-term C and D relate to capital markets.

**28 B**

Nominal rates incorporate both real rates and inflation. In periods of high inflation nominal rates may be high despite low real rates.

**29 D**

$$\text{Multiplier} = \frac{1}{\text{mps}} = \frac{1}{(1 - \text{mpc})}$$

**30 A**

Recessionary pressure will reduce demand pull inflation and may even cause prices to fall.

Demand in the local economy is low, reducing imports and improving the trade balance. The low demand also causes more unemployment and a fall in national output.

**31**

| Definition of unemployment | Type of unemployment |
|---|---|
| (i) Unemployment that occurs in particular industries and arises from long-term changes in the patterns of demand and supply | Structural unemployment |
| (ii) Unemployment associated with industries or regions where the demand for labour and wage rates regularly rise and fall over the year | Seasonal unemployment |

**32** **A**

Unemployment may be a consequence of a fall in economic activity but is not the cause of it.

**33** **C**

Supply side policies focus on increasing aggregate supply.

**34**

| Type of tax | Direct | Indirect |
|---|---|---|
| Income tax | ✓ | |
| Value added tax | | ✓ |
| Corporation tax | ✓ | |
| National insurance (social security tax) | ✓ | |

**35** A negative supply shock would shift the aggregate supply curve to the left and cause the rate of inflation to increase. However, the level of national output would fall. An expansionary fiscal policy would shift the aggregate demand curve to the right leading to a rise in both the level of national output and the rate of inflation.

**36** **B**

High tariffs and other trade barriers restrict globalisation.

**37** **A**

The collapse of a single market would make it harder for the countries involved to do business with each other rather than easier.

**38** **C and D**

Invisible trade is part of the current account so would be included in the deficit. Flows on profits and interest on capital are part of the invisible balance.

**39 C**

| Product | d | $d^2$ |
|---|---|---|
| V | 0.5 | 0.25 |
| W | –2 | 4 |
| X | 4 | 16 |
| Y | –2.5 | 6.25 |
| Z | 0 | 0 |

$$r = 1 - \frac{6 \times \Sigma d^2}{n \times (n^2 - 1)}$$

$\Sigma d^2 = 26.5$

$$r = 1 - \frac{6 \times 26.5}{5 \times (5^2 - 1)} = 1 - \frac{159}{120} = -0.325 = -0.33$$

**40 C**

Interest rates in single currency zones may be higher than those of countries outside the zone and will be influences by policy objectives within the zone, such as countering inflation.

**41 B and D**

A will lower inflation and C will leave inflation unchanged. B and D lead to increased investment and a growing aggregate demand. If demand is rising but supply cannot as the country is close to full employment, the consequence is price rises.

**42 B**

Floating exchange rate systems have a natural tendency to eliminate balance of payments deficits and surpluses.

**43 A**

Quotas reduce supply, so result in higher prices (think of a supply curve shifting to the left and what that does to the equilibrium point).

**44 D**

Borrowers and those who hold assets gain from inflation. For borrowers, the real value of their debt falls over time. For those who hold assets, the realisable value of the asset increases over time.

**45 B**

Dividend yield

= Share price beginning of year \$1.20

Dividend paid 12c

= 10%

**46 D**

No need to deduct interest from PAT as it will already have been deducted.

$$\text{Earnings per share} = \frac{\$20{,}000}{100{,}000}$$

= 20c

**47 A**

A government subsidy would shift the supply curve to the right since it makes the product cheaper.

**48 D**

Ordinary shares, debentures and convertible bonds are all examples of long-term capital.

**49 D**

Import quotas, import tariffs and export subsidies are all examples of protectionism.

**50 D**

An increase in imports, an increase in taxes and a reduction in government expenditure would all constitute a withdrawal from the circular flow of income.

**51 D**

The exchange rate would rise in the short-term as foreign investors are attracted to local deposits. As borrowing becomes more difficult, non-financial assets such as housing would become more difficult to acquire and as demand for them falls, so will the price. Rising interest would encourage saving and discourage spending, leading to lower aggregate demand and less inflationary pressure. If the central bank was to increase interest rates, consumer expenditure would fall and savings would rise.

**52 B**

For the economy to be in equilibrium, the overall levels of injections (government spending, investment and exports) and withdrawals (taxation, savings and imports) should be equal.

It is not necessary for the individual opposing values (e.g. imports and exports) to be equal. Even if, say, government spending and taxation were at equal levels, the other components of injections and withdrawals may not be and therefore the economy as a whole may not be in equilibrium.

**53 A**

B, C and D are examples of internal economies of scale (economics of scale that accrue to the firm because the firm itself gets bigger).

**54 A and E**

Outsourcing increases transaction costs within the organisation – it does not reduce them. It may be difficult for P to bring functions back in house later as her business will be likely to have lost the internal skills and staffing when it is outsourced to a third party.

**55 103.8**

$$\text{Weighted average index} = \frac{\sum(\text{weighting} \times \text{index})}{\sum\text{weighting}}$$

$$\text{Weighted average index} = \frac{[(3 \times 105) + (2 \times 103) + (1 \times 102)]}{(3 + 2 + 1)} = 103.8$$

**56 561**

For the 1st quarter of 2017, t = 17 and trend Y = 462 + 0.34 × 17 = 467.8 (to 1 d.p.)

Prediction = trend prediction increased by 20% = 467.8 × 1.20 = 561

**57 B**

An ogive doesn't have bars. A bar chart looks like a histogram but in a bar chart the height of the bar represents the frequency. In a histogram this is only the case if the classes are of equal width. In general, the area of the bar in a histogram represents class frequency.

**58 D**

The Australian customer has been invoiced in NZD so there is no forex risk associated with the receipt.

**59 C and E**

Economic risk, in the exchange rate risk context, is the variation in the value of a business due to unexpected changes in exchange rates. It is the long-term version of transaction risk which is the risk of exchange rates changing between the date of the transaction and the settlement date.

The spot market is one in you can buy and sell currency now.

**60 B**

8 years annuity at 10%, from cumulative present value table = 5.335

NPV = (1,200 × 5.335) – 6,200 = 6,402 – 6,200 = 202.